DATE DUE

MAY 1 1 2010	
MAY 2 5 2010	
AUG 1 4 2010	
ILL 1/15	
ILL 8/15	
2017	

GAYLORD   PRINTED IN U.S.A.

Kids on the Trail!

Hiking with Children in the Adirondacks

Rose Rivezzi & David Trithart

Adirondack Mountain Club
Lake George, New York

ADIRONDACK
MOUNTAIN CLUB

Conservation • Education • Recreation

Published by the Adirondack Mountain Club, Inc.
814 Goggins Road, Lake George, New York 12845-4117
Visit our Web site at www.adk.org

Printed in the United States of America
01 02 03 04 05 06 07 08 09   10 9 8 7 6 5 4 3

Photographs by the authors unless noted otherwise.
Illustrations by Albert Trithart, except pp. 46 and 147 by Willie Trithart.

Book design and typography by Christopher Kuntze
Cover photograph © 1997 Carl Heilman II

The quotation on page 13 is excerpted with permission of HarperCollins publishers from *A Sense of Wonder* by Rachel Carson, © 1956 by Rachel L. Carson, copyright © renewed 1984 by Roger Christie.

Note: the use of the information in this book is at the sole risk of the user.

Library of Congress Cataloging-in-Publication Data
Rivezzi, Rose, 1958–
         Kids on the trail! : hiking with children in the Adirondacks /
    Rose Rivezzi and David Trithart.
               p.   cm.
         Includes bibliographical references and index.
         ISBN 0-935272-91-7 (pbk.)
         1. Hiking—New York (State)—Adirondack Mountains—Guidebooks.
    2. Family recreation—New York (State)—Adirondack Mountains—
    Guidebooks. 3. Adirondack Mountains (N.Y.)—Guidebooks.
    I. Trithart, David, 1948–   . II. Title
    GV199.42.N652A3472   1997
    796.51'09747'5—dc21
                                                            97-36706
                                                            CIP

The Adirondack Mountain Club (ADK) is dedicated to the protection and responsible recreational use of the New York State Forest Preserve, parks, and other wild lands and waters. The Club, founded in 1922, is a member-directed organization committed to public service and stewardship. ADK employs a balanced approach to outdoor recreation, advocacy, environmental education and natural resource conservation.

*This book is dedicated
to our children*

ALBERT *&* WILLIE

*and other hikers of
their generation.*

We hope they will join the individuals and organizations of past and present who have worked to preserve wilderness within the Adirondack Park. The Park is truly a special place, one that we hope will be enjoyed by our children's children and generations beyond.

The question is not what you look at,
but what you see.

HENRY DAVID THOREAU

ACKNOWLEDGMENTS

We are fortunate to have so many friends, young and old, who share our love of being on the trail. Not only did we have great company on so many of our outings but we also had the warm hospitality of those who live in other sections of the Park, and the advice and suggestions so many offered. A heartfelt thanks for the support and encouragement we felt from all these people and from our families as we worked on this project.

We had much help and support in the writing of this book. We appreciate the time and effort of the many individuals who read our drafts and offered their suggestions. Warm thanks also to Andrea Masters, the Publications Committee, and the staff at ADK headquarters who helped us with our questions and gave us the nudge to attempt this book. Our hikes took us to areas of the Park where we had never been and enhanced our appreciation for the gift we have in this tract of land.

And one last thank you to our two favorite hiking companions, Albert, 10, and Willie, 8. We love being with them on the trail and we look forward to many more happy outings together.

Rose Rivezzi
David Trithart

We Welcome Your Letters!

ADK and its authors make every effort to keep our guidebooks up to date, however, trail conditions are always changing. If you note an error or discrepancy, or if you wish to forward a suggestion, we welcome your input. Please write the Adirondack Mountain Club, Attn: Publications, citing book title, year of your edition (see copyright page), trail number, page number, and date of your observation. Thanks for your help.

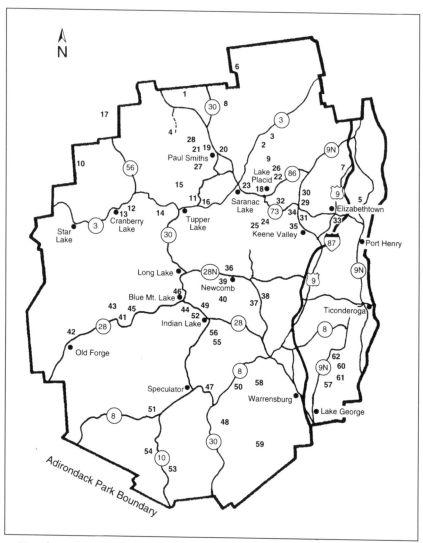

Numbers 1 through 62 correspond to hike descriptions in this book

Contents

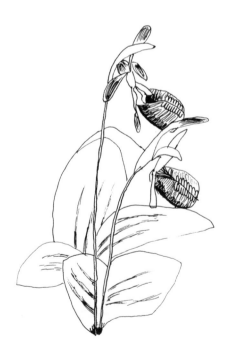

Before You Lace Up

A child's world is fresh and new and beautiful, full of wonder and excitement. It is our misfortune that for most of us that clear-eyed vision, that true instinct for what is beautiful and awe-inspiring, is dimmed and even lost before we reach adulthood. . . .

If a child is to keep alive his inborn sense of wonder . . . he needs the companionship of at least one adult who can share it, rediscovering with him the joy, excitement and mystery of the world we live in.

RACHEL CARSON

THE ADIRONDACK PARK abounds with occasions and places to inspire wonder—a secluded waterfall, the flutelike call of a hidden thrush, the delicate color and design of a lady's slipper, the chittery din as hundreds of beetles march through the brittle leafy ground cover, the perfume of the resin-filled sacs on the bark of the balsam fir. We are fortunate to have such expanses of wild lands to help us instill a sense of wonder in our children. In this book we refer to children and their parents, but as Rachel Carson expressed, the hiking companion does not have to be a parent. Aunts, uncles, grandparents, friends, and neighbors may be the adults in a child's life who nurture that sense of wonder.

Adults who like to hike don't need to stop hiking just because they become parents. It may be necessary to modify the kinds of hikes chosen, but the basic joys of getting out into the wilds need not be abandoned. Look for hikes that are not too difficult for children, but which have the features that attracted you to hiking in the first place. The views, trailside streams, waterfalls, lakes, cliffs, wildlife, and sense of accomplishment in meeting a challenge can all be enjoyed by children. For those adults who have not hiked before, hiking with children is a great way for all of you to start small as you learn about hiking and gain experience in the natural world.

Children of any age can enjoy the outdoor experience afforded by hiking. That experience changes as children grow and develop new interests and abilities. In the following pages we note special considerations for hiking with infants and toddlers, young children (2–5 years) and older children (6–12 years).

This guide describes sixty-two hikes distributed throughout the Adirondack Park. Included are many beautiful hikes within the High Peaks region of the Park. Although a number of the higher peaks—those over 4000 (1219 m) feet in elevation—are within the ability of many children, they are not included in this guide. They are described at length in other publications and, partly as a result, these trails are overused. It is important for more people to become aware that great hiking experiences are not limited to the best known sections of the Park. We've only begun to look at possible places to go with children. By sharing with you how we chose what we thought would be good children's hikes, we hope that you will be able to move beyond this guidebook to select other hikes on your own.

We talked with other people who hiked with children. We found out about their favorite places. Hikers always seem to be ready to talk of their adventures and misadventures and much information can be gained from their experiences. We spent time looking at maps and reading guidebooks. The Adirondack Mountain Club (ADK) series of books has lots of information. We considered hike length, amount of elevation gain, and features that would be appealing to children. Information about newer trails, such as the Silver Lake Bog Walk, sometimes is included in publications from The Nature Conservancy or other organizations.

WE HAVE USED ONE OF THE FOLLOWING FOUR ICONS TO CATEGORIZE EACH HIKE:

 Fairly level walk of a
short to moderate distance

 Short hike with significant elevation gain
or longer hike with moderate elevation gain

 More challenging hike due to longer length
and/or greater elevation gain

 Wilderness camping
possibility

For each hike we give the round-trip distance and amount of elevation gain, but we do not attempt to give estimated times. The pace of hikes with children will vary greatly. A four-year-old out on a first hike may need an hour to cover less than a mile, whereas a rambunctious eight-year-old may complete the same hike in thirty minutes. We've seen children surpass the abilities of out-of-shape adults and teens. An observant hiker will also need more time on the trail. A conservative rule of thumb for an adult would be to allow one hour per mile-and-a-half with an added half hour for each 1000 ft (305 m) of ascent. Plan more time when hiking with children and remember that a mile walk in town is not the same as a mile on the trail.

Before each section of hikes we've included a selected list of nearby attractions to help you plan other pleasurable stops on your excursions. You can obtain additional information from tourism brochures, or from guides such as *The Adirondack Book: A Complete Guide* by Elizabeth Folwell.

We have tried to provide clear trailhead descriptions, but we strongly recommend a good road atlas to help you locate trailheads. We found the *New York State Atlas and Gazetteer* by the DeLorme Mapping Company to be an invaluable tool. We have tried to provide accurate trail descriptions, and page maps for many of the hikes are included, but note that storm damage, beaver flooding, and other forces can divert or obscure a trail, so be alert to this possibility. We recommend you carry a compass and trail maps and feel comfortable using them. The Adirondack Mountain Club sells trail maps and they are also included in the Forest Preserve guidebook series (see Selected References).

Some of our hike descriptions tell what made a hike special for us. These descriptions may give you ideas of the sorts of things to point out to children during your walks. Each hike will be special to you and your child for so many different reasons. You will also find that the stories you tell about your hikes increase their value and come to define the hike in the child's memory. Keep your eyes open and your wonderment heartfelt. Make each hike your own.

Why Hike with Children?

Our reality has changed. The media have become 3-dimensional, inescapable, omnivorous, and self-referring—a closed system that seems, for many of the kids, to answer all their questions.

DAVID DENBY, *The New Yorker*

In a time and place becoming saturated with "mediated" experience—electronic, virtual, high-speed—what can be the value of an activity as seemingly anachronistic as hiking? Can there be value precisely because hiking is an activity so at odds with the dominant and pervasive kinds of reality of our daily lives? What can hiking and camping mean for the development of a child? To quote David Abram:

> Direct sensuous reality, in all its more-than-human mystery, remains the sole solid touchstone for an experiential world now inundated with electronically-generated vistas and engineered pleasures; only in regular contact with the tangible ground and sky can we learn how to orient and navigate in the multiple dimensions that now claim us.

Many people are beginning to realize the importance of personal experience with nature to achieve an awareness of our existence as part of nature. Even the sounds of nature—rivers, birds, forests, wind—nourish us with their cadences. What sounds do we call our children's attention to first, but the sounds of animals?

As parents, we want to help our children to appreciate nature and to see themselves as connected to it. Books and discussion could be one way of doing this, but helping them be comfortable with and appreciative of the natural world around them is doubtless more effective. We begin with forays into our own back yards, noticing the seasonal changes, the sky, the birds, and the insects in our daily world. It may not be until a child has an experience with a world so different from the "civilized" one he or she knows that an understanding begins to develop of what will be lost if our wilderness areas continue to be threatened. Our hope is that our children will want to carry on the struggle to preserve what remains of our wilderness when they become adults. We don't lecture as we hike, but we hope that they will come to appreciate the value of the natural world. As David W. Orr notes:

> We are never more than one generation away from losing the idea of forests as places of wildness and ecstasy, mystery and renewal, as well as the knowledge of their importance for human survival . . . But the power behind the idea of decent forests depends on the experience of decent forests, not on secondhand, bookish abstractions.

Hiking with children also allows for lots of family time while on the trail. There are no "technological distractions" such as TVs, phones, or computers. There is plenty of time for thinking, talking, and sharing. Our children ask many questions while we hike and our attempts to answer them cause us to revisit issues about which we haven't thought for so long. Their questions about the natural world challenge us to explain things in ways they will understand and also bring us to see things we have missed while hiking at an adult pace with adult eyes.

Making Hiking Enjoyable

Enjoyable experiences make it more likely that your child will want to continue hiking. Much that you like about hiking, your child will enjoy, too. A good trail provides regular stimulus and will include intermediate goals or highlights to refresh enthusiasm. Take your cues from the children themselves, but try to set the tone with your own enthusiasm and eagerness to note anything of interest.

Learn What Your Children Enjoy about Hiking

Some people think that children are slow to develop an appreciation of scenery. The young child may be more interested in small trailside features, the near-at-hand, rather than the broad panorama. Rather than resist this tendency, let it be a way to reawaken your own awareness. Temper your desire to "cover ground" and you may uncover small wonders.

For some people, part of the essence of hiking is to get away from crowds, to experience the silence and sounds of the wilderness. Others enjoy hiking as a social event, the conviviality of people sharing an activity they all enjoy. Children may fall into either of these camps, or indeed, be able to enjoy both aspects. Some trails are better suited for quiet wilderness experiences, others for socializing. Generally speaking, the High Peaks trails are more heavily traveled. Certain peaks and trails outside of the High Peaks area are also quite popular and may be busy, especially on summer weekends.

Weekdays are usually quieter. We recommend that you do not insist on only hikes where you can be alone in the wilderness, even if those are your favorites. Children may be energized by the presence of other hikers and encouraged by seeing others who enjoy hiking. At another stage in their lives they may come to appreciate what you find in solitude.

You may discover that children enjoy aspects of hiking that do not appeal to you. Blowdown on the trail is exciting because of the challenge of jumping and ducking one's way through the tangle of branches and limbs. Our children wouldn't hear of a suggestion to go around it. The sounds and feel of mud are also irresistible to children. Some other trail features that appeal to children, and which often slow progress toward the destination, are rock hopping over streams and across wet sections of trail, ladders, long bridges (especially the narrow treacherous kind), and bare rock scrambles. Keep safety and trail etiquette in mind, but let children enjoy the hike in their own way.

But we are not totally at odds with our children. Wildflowers, wildlife, rock formations, views from open ledges and ridges, water of any kind—these can be appreciated equally by all. The most successful hike is one in which the joys of discovery are as much the child's as yours. Your children will point out what they find interesting. The response they get from you, which can include information to extend their understanding of the world, is critical to maintaining their level of enthusiasm. It doesn't matter if you are not an expert naturalist. As Joseph Cornell points out in his guide, *Sharing Nature with Children*, "Don't feel badly about not knowing names. . . . Look. Ask questions. Guess. Have fun! As your children begin to develop an attunement with nature, your relationship with them will evolve from one of teacher and fellow-student to one of fellow-adventurer."

Create Positive Memories

Many of our hikes are remembered with special descriptive names or recalled by particular events that made them special. Rather than, "Remember when we hiked to the Gulf Brook lean-to?" we'll say, "Remember the lean-to where you went skinny-dipping in the cold water?" Photographs help trigger great memories.

Were our children always happy when they hiked? Of course not. There was an occasional bad mood or squabble with a brother or friend. In those cases, a talk afterwards as to how the problem could be avoided next time, or a reminder of the great things about the hike, helped to turn things around. On one hike, a five-year-old friend was with us, and there were some sad feelings when he was not chosen to lead the hike out. His mother talked about the hike with him at the end of the day, during his bath, highlighting all the nice things that had happened. It was the first time he had picked up a frog! Help your children form positive memories.

Are We There Yet?

Remember, you set the tone for your child's expectations. The main purpose of your hike is to acquaint your child with the outdoors or a new trail—and to have a good time. Don't be tempted to readjust the focus to suit your desire to conquer a mountain peak or achieve a certain landmark.

The following tips help keep any hike enjoyable.

BEFORE
- Plan a hike with your children's abilities in mind
- Let children know what to expect from the hike
- Plan the hike as part of a trip or in conjunction with another activity

DURING
- Give food and drink before your children experience energy lows or real thirst
- Take frequent rests
- Give lots of encouragement and praise children's efforts
- Make up games along the way; sing songs; tell stories
- Offer rewards and incentives (a special treat at the midway point or once back at the car)
- Remember children may derive pleasure in ways different from an adult

AFTER
- Take pictures and reminisce about favorite outings; remember the good points
- Review the hike with a map before you; mark the trail using colored pencils or markers; display the map
- Create a list of hikes with dates and comments about special experiences or features

Give Lots of Help and Encouragement

Children need to know how proud you are of their efforts. They feel great when told they've far exceeded your expectations or when they see how much farther they've walked, compared to a previous hike. Recording completed hikes can provide a sense of accomplishment. Along the trail, when possible, point out the mountain about to be climbed or just climbed.

Be prepared to help with difficult trail sections, such as brook crossings and steep sections (up and down). Holding a hand where there are drop-offs is a must, but just holding a hand now and then can be nice, too.

Have Fun while Hiking

Even for the older child, the motivation derived from pursuit of a long-delayed goal, such as arrival at the summit or final destination, is less than for an adult. Even the parent who believes strongly in the value of learning "delayed gratification" should recognize the need for shorter-term rewards. Most parents will develop their own repertoire of motivators for times when their children hit that occasional low.

We played lots of games while we hiked. The kids remember very fondly a hike on which their uncle hiked ahead. A while later, they discovered a string of M&M's along the trail. As they stopped to investigate, out he jumped. On another hike on a breezy fall day, they spent lots of time trying to catch the leaves as they drifted down. The leaves were "bombs," but they brought tremendous good luck if they could be caught while in the air. We also played counting games in which we counted all the frogs we saw or all the orange things, etc. We sang songs, made up silly verses, and spent hours imagining what things would be like if . . . .

We are continually surprised at where their thoughts lead us. A good part of one hike was spent answering one child's question of "How can there be nothing?" and part of another imagining the largest number for which we had a word and if the grains of sand could come close to that number. Storytelling and retelling anecdotes from our own experiences also help the miles to pass more quickly. It's a great time to talk with and listen to your children since there are few distractions except the natural ones that catch your eye.

Spend Time to Mentally Prepare for a Hike

Mental preparation is second nature to adults. We anticipate the sustained effort that will be needed for the climb. Children often do better if they know what to expect on a hike. They should be warned if there will be some steep sections that may be difficult, and that they may have tired legs or hit energy lows. Remind them of the rewards to be gained by persevering. They will begin to "think like a hiker." Soon they will appreciate that sense of pride that hikers have as they tell their stories of how hard it all was, yet worth the effort. Of course, we try to make the experience as pleasant as possible, but hiking involves physical exertion. Recall the other hikes you've done in which the goal was worth the effort. In anticipating a hike, make it sound exciting, but don't build it up to the point that reality comes as a major disappointment.

Use Rewards

Nutritious food is important to maintain energy levels on longer hikes. Snacks along the way can be energy boosters and motivators if distributed cleverly. Great snacks include dried fruits, GORP (which goes beyond good old raisins and peanuts with our addition of chocolate, sunflower seeds, almonds, dried cherries, etc.), and granola bars. But our all-time favorite motivator is the "power pill," a piece of candy for times when energy runs low. "It looks like we need some energy. Power pills are coming out at the next big rock." Off they go to await the treat. Candy should not be used to alleviate hunger, but as that little extra we all love.

Combine Your Hike with Other Pleasurable Outings

Many of our hiking adventures were combined with some other pleasurable outing. As one of our children noted, why would you drive 100 miles to hike one or two miles? Well, we don't. Hikes with children, which are usually shorter forays, can be done on the way to or from somewhere else, or planned as an opportunity to meet with distant friends, or as part of a vacation trip when many days are being spent in one area. There may also be other nearby places of interest to make a whole day's outing. Perhaps there is a fish hatchery or a public beach not too far away. Meals were often part of our trips. Think about that great dessert into which you will sink your teeth, or which flavor ice cream you want, or how those pancakes will taste for breakfast after a night in the woods. There are museums and historic sights scattered throughout the Adirondacks as well as more commercial attractions which many children enjoy. Many small towns have special events and festivals throughout the year. Attending these events can be combined with a hiking outing.

Comfort and Safety

Visitors to the Adirondacks should be aware that conditions in the mountains can be quite different from surrounding areas. Spring comes later, winds and rain may arrive unexpectedly, and deep snow can be encountered long after it has disappeared at lower elevations.

Parents must consider the safety and comfort of their children when hiking. An adult may tolerate discomfort due to insects, hunger, or weather as the price to be paid for other satisfactions. For children, immediate conditions are most important. Adults need to keep children on the trail so that no one gets lost and dangers are avoided, since these concerns are unlikely to occur to children. In this section we discuss areas in which foresight can help avoid uncomfortable situations as well as potentially dangerous ones. Prompt emergency assistance on the trail may be very difficult or impossible to obtain. You have to rely on good planning, the equipment you brought with you, and your common sense.

Safety Reminders

- Hike within your capabilities
- Turn back short of your goal when necessary
- Allow enough time to hike
- Take plenty of water to drink
- Tell someone where you're going
- Sign in at the trail register
- Dress in layers and anticipate changing conditions
- Wear synthetic or wool fabrics
- Keep to the trail
- Use common sense

Do Not Go Beyond Your Own Comfort Level

It's a good idea to be comfortable with the outdoors yourself before bringing children onto the trails. If you know what to expect, you can more effectively plan a safe outing for your child. If your own hiking experience has been limited, you may feel more comfortable hiking with someone with trail experience or joining a group hike. The Adirondack Mountain Club chapter in your area may offer hikes for families. Start with nature walks around home and then short hikes as you gain experience.

If you begin to feel uncomfortable or frightened, or have misgivings about a situation on the trail, you need to decide what can be done to eliminate the risk or danger. You may need to turn around without reaching your goal. The amount of daylight remaining, weather conditions, winds, the distance still to travel, and energy levels must be considered. Be conservative in making decisions when you have children with you. You can take more risks when you are alone or with other adults.

When our oldest son was six months old, we decided to do a cross-country ski outing of about six miles round-trip. He was as happy as could be going in. His usual nursing time came when we reached our turnaround point, where we planned to eat lunch. He refused to nurse, so we started back, expecting an easy three miles on a slightly downhill grade. It began to snow heavily. The large flakes were landing on his face and there was nothing we could do about it. He cried all the way out. He eagerly nursed in the car and seems to have suffered no long-lasting animosity towards back country travel. We reached our destination, but we did not linger for lunch and we quickened our pace on the way out. Use your common sense to do what's best.

A decision to turn back can make you feel as if you've failed. You may be in a situation where the children want to continue, but you feel it is unwise. Take charge of the situation. Calmly explain why you have made the decision to turn around and stick with your decision. Don't make the child feel as if he or she was the reason the trip was not completed.

One time we had hiked a few miles with our frame packs. We dropped off our packs and had a snack at the lean-to where we planned to camp, then started up the mountain. We were eager and thought we'd have plenty of time before dinner. Well, we were wrong. The trail was steeper than we had anticipated and we started later in the day than usual. We didn't have enough daylight to take an extended rest, and the boys were tired from an outing the previous day. They did not want to turn back, but we felt it would be unwise to go on. We explained that there would not be enough daylight and said that we were too tired to go on. We shared stories of other times when, hiking without children, we had to turn back. The mountain would always be there for another attempt in better conditions. We had a happy dinner at our lean-to and resolved to try the peak another time. It was a good lesson in not letting our goals get the better of us.

Before You Start Your Hike

Let others know where you will be hiking and when you expect to return. Use the trail registers to log in and out. These wooden boxes, present at most trailheads, contain logbooks for hikers to record their names and destinations. Not only does this help monitor trail use, but it may be invaluable in locating you if there is an emergency.

There are many factors to consider when deciding on the adult-to-child ratio. One parent may feel very comfortable hiking with two or more children if the intended trail is well traveled or if the children are older and she knows their hiking capabilities. On longer hikes, which may be in less traveled areas of the Park, we felt most comfortable with at least two adults. If there were a serious injury or other emergency, a second adult would be invaluable. Imagine possible problems and have solutions in mind. What would I do if I sprained an ankle? What would I do if one of my children sprained an ankle? Emergencies are the exception rather than the rule, but when we hike with children, forethought is especially important.

Allow plenty of time for a hike. Choose one within your capabilities and that of your children. Wear a watch and check the time when you begin the hike. Keep track of how long you've been on the trail so that you can allow enough daylight time

Ralph Keating

Megan Keating, 5, and her brother Erik, 2. Megan chose a white dress and frilly socks for the hike; her father Ralph chose to accept her decision, carrying her raincoat and extra warm clothing for changing circumstances.

for the return. Delays caused by an injury or losing the trail can occur. A flashlight is important if you get caught on the trail after dark, but a better alternative may be a headlamp which leaves your hands free. Always check batteries before leaving home and bring spares.

A first aid kit is also essential. A basic kit contains gauze pads, bandages, adhesive tape, an ace bandage, tweezers, scissors, and first aid cream. Put together your own kit or look for commercial kits in neatly organized little pouches, available in stores or through the American Red Cross. Basic first aid information may also be helpful.

What Should You Take?

HIKING ESSENTIALS:
Water
Guidebook
Map
Food
Extra clothing (socks; extra layer for warmth)
Rain jacket
First aid kit
Toilet paper and trowel
Pocketknife
Flashlight or headlamp
Watch
Whistle
Compass
Matches
Moleskin

IF APPLICABLE:
Diapers (and a plastic bag for soiled ones)
Child carrier
Sunscreen
Bug repellent and/or head nets
Hats and mittens

OPTIONAL:
Hand lens
Field guides
Binoculars
Camera

Sun and Bug Protection

There are times when you will need to consider protection from bugs when hiking in the Adirondacks. Hiking in the month of June usually means dealing with blackflies. Mosquitoes and deerflies are usually present during the summer. Even if bugs are not a problem during a day hike, evening may be another story.

N, N-diethyl-meta-toluamide (commonly known as DEET) is a pretty strong chemical best used sparingly, but it is effective. The brands of repellent on the market contain varying amounts of DEET. Read the directions carefully and never apply insect repellent to a child's hands, which then travel to the mouth and eyes. Applying the repellent to a bandanna or hat brim rather than to the skin is a good idea. Only apply it when you know that bugs are a problem and rinse it off well upon returning home. Pediatricians recommend that DEET not be used on children under six months of age. More natural repellents containing citronella and other oils are also available.

Measures to reduce the need for chemical repellents include covering up as much as possible with lightweight, long-sleeved shirts and long pants. You can also wear bug netting, which is easily carried in a pack and can be slipped over a hat when needed. Long clothing offers protection against ticks carrying Lyme disease. Tick checks after a romp in the woods should be done before the after-hiking bath or shower.

Sun may not be a concern on shaded trails (remember, however, that trees leaf out later at higher elevations), but it should be a consideration if the destination is a summit or other open and unshaded area. Many very effective sunscreens and lotions are available. Hats also help. Chapstick with sun protection for lips should also be used. Use the products that work best for you when it comes to sun and bug protection.

Food and Water

Make sure you carry enough food and water. For a typical day hike, one adult can carry a backpack with the essentials (see sidebar), while the other carries a fanny pack with two water bottle holders. This is convenient because the kids can take water whenever needed without stopping to dig the bottle out of a pack. Screw-top plastic bottles work the best because they don't leak. We've tried water bottles made for bikes, but children tend to chew the nipple top and often these bottles leak if not kept upright.

You will need to drink more water while hiking than you do at home. We typically plan on a pint of water per hiker for an outing of a few hours. More water is needed for longer outings. Children may not realize how thirsty they are getting. Encourage them to drink lots of water, especially on days when it is not very hot and the need may not be as apparent to them.

Drinking plenty of water reduces the chances of hyperthermia, or heatstroke. Warning signs are complaints of feeling sick, dizzy, confused, or faint. The person is flushed with hot, dry skin. The brain mechanism that regulates body temperature stops functioning and body temperatures may rise quickly. Heat exhaustion results from insufficient liquids or salts. There is excessive sweating and the skin becomes pale and clammy. In both cases, move the person to the coolest spot available. Use a wet cloth to cool the person and give him or her fluids to drink.

Do not drink the water from lakes or streams unless you first pass it through a water purifier, add purifying tablets, or boil it for two to three minutes. Many Adirondack water sources have been contaminated with a parasite known as *Giardia lamblia*. This intestinal parasite causes a disease called giardiasis or "beaver fever." It can be spread by any warm-blooded mammal, such as the common beaver, when infected feces wash into the water. If you or your children experience recurrent intestinal problems after an outing on which you've drunk untreated water, consult your doctor, telling her of the possible cause.

If children say they're hungry, stop for a nutritious, high energy snack (not candy). Kids cannot always delay eating until they reach the planned lunch site, as adults can. Take foods that will satisfy their hunger and that you know they will like. The following is a partial list of good snack and lunch items:

— crackers and cheese or pepperoni
— apples with peanut butter or cheese
— simple sandwiches that aren't messy
— rice cakes (can be bulky, but they're very lightweight)
— carrot and celery sticks
— dried fruit
— cookies and granola bars
— pretzels or corn chips
— bagels
— something special as a surprise (usually chocolate for our family)

Stopping to eat on a regular basis is a good idea. It provides a chance to rest and helps keep energy up.

Clothing

Weather can change quickly in the Adirondacks. You may also be on the trail longer than you expected because of delays, injury, or an inaccurate estimation of the time needed for the hike. Temperatures drop as the sun goes down. Summits will be cooler than lower elevations and often windy. Appropriate clothing selection is essential for both comfort and safety.

Hypothermia occurs when the body's temperature drops dangerously low. It is a year-round possibility. During prolonged exposure to cool temperatures, more body heat may be lost than generated, if you are not dressed properly. Air temperatures need not be below freezing for hypothermia to occur. A sudden soaking rain or a fall in a brook combined with a rising wind or cool summit breeze can put a person at risk. Children are especially vulnerable. Once energy reserves have been used, the fall in body temperature will cause a gradual physical and mental slowing down. Clumsiness, drowsiness, and confusion are signs of hypothermia. Not only are the hands and feet cold, but so is the abdominal area.

The best prevention is dressing properly. Dress in layers of wool or synthetic materials which wick moisture away from the skin. Cotton clothing is not recommended for hiking. When cotton gets wet from rain or sweat, it stays wet for a long time, drawing heat away from the body.

Layered clothing works much better than just one warm jacket. A polypropylene or other synthetic fabric layer closest to the body, followed by another shirt or sweater, is a good base. A jacket or vest of polar fleece or wool adds even more warmth. Fleece can be bulky to carry, but is warm for its weight and very quick to dry. If it's windy or rainy, a waterproof shell should be the final layer. Coated rain jackets are usually adequate. Gore-Tex®, which is breathable as well as waterproof, is probably the best material but may be too expensive. Rain pants or rain chaps may also be nice, especially for walks after it's rained and the brush lining a narrow trail is wet. Large plastic bags can also serve as rain gear in a pinch.

If a member of your party is suffering from hypothermia, act quickly. The *American Medical Association Family Medical Guide* advises that you do what you can to warm the person. Additional dry covering, a warm drink, or warming with another person's body heat may help. If the hypothermia is severe, treatment must be gradual; too rapid an application of heat can cause sudden enlargement of blood vessels at the body surface. If this happens, a rush of blood into the dilated vessels may rob vital inner organs of the blood they need in order to continue functioning. Anyone who has suffered hypothermia should be checked by a physician.

Children can become quite warm while walking or climbing. Unzip jackets or remove a layer before children become sweaty, which can cool them down too quickly. Hats help regulate temperature, too. Taking a hat off may be all that's needed to cool a child down or putting one on may be all they need to start warming up. Polar fleece or wool hats work well. Bring along gloves or mittens, too. Lightweight synthetic glove liners may be enough on a milder fall day. Warm socks of either wool or partly synthetic fibers work well to keep feet warm. Make sure that heavier socks are not too thick for the boot or shoe the child is wearing, which will then make boots too tight. A thin, synthetic liner sock underneath a pair of heavier socks will help prevent blisters.

Older children are able to tell you if they're too hot or cold. If you think your infant may be cold, check the nape of the neck, arms, or trunk. These areas are better indicators of body temperature than hands or feet. Remember that an infant or toddler who is being carried will not be as warm as you are while you are hiking. On the other hand, if an observant toddler is walking at his or her own pace, you may need to dress more warmly than usual, as you will not be moving quickly.

In colder weather, watch for frostbite. Most commonly affected are fingers, toes, and face. Frostbitten parts remain white if gently pinched and feel hard and cold. Warm the affected body part at the first sign of frostbite. Hands can be placed in an armpit or between your legs. Do not rub a frostbitten area, as the friction can cause further damage. Dress for the weather conditions to prevent frostbite.

Besides the extra clothing brought along on the hike, always leave extra clothing, socks, and shoes in the car, which can make the ride home much more comfortable.

Footwear

All hikers want happy feet. Young hikers under the age of five who are only hiking a short distance, or who are being carried some of the way, do just fine in a comfortable pair of sneakers, as long as they provide good support. We don't suggest buying hiking boots if you only hike once a year. As children begin to hike more often and cover more ground, they'll want more rugged footwear that provides more support and holds up to trail conditions better.

Many kinds of hiking boots are available for children. More expensive does not always mean better. In general, look for a boot that is lightweight and, most important, comfortable. Make sure there is enough toe room. Have the child stand on a downward incline when trying on the boots, since some of their hiking time will be spent going down steep sections where toes are pushed to the front of the boot. Make sure the boots are not too loose in the back or they will rub against the back of the foot. When trying on boots, have the child wear the type of socks that will be worn while hiking.

Boots should be worn around the house and for walks around town before wearing them on the trails. It's never a good idea to wear new boots on a hike. If a child complains of a "hot spot" on the foot, stop. Remove the boot and see if there is something rubbing. It may be a good idea to place a bandage on the trouble spot. Lamb's wool or moleskin is handy to have in your pack to cushion tender spots.

Sanitation

For a child who has never used anything but an indoor toilet, going to the bathroom outside may be a strange idea. We carry some toilet paper in a plastic bag in our pack. Move off the trail, making sure you are at least 150 ft. (46 m) away from streams or ponds. If the child seems afraid, accompany him or her. When urinating in the woods, little boys have little difficulty. Little girls may need some help keeping their balance as they squat and with keeping all their garments safely out of the way. When eliminating solid wastes, you will need to help a child find a spot where you can make a hole about six inches deep to bury the waste. A site near a tree or large rock that can also be used for support works well. Carry along a small trowel to ensure you can make a hole six inches deep, or look for a sturdy stick on the ground to use as a digging tool. When done, make sure all toilet paper and waste are well covered. Trails with camping areas may have outhouses. Use them whenever possible.

Trail Safety

The adage "An ounce of prevention is worth a pound of cure" certainly applies to trail safety for children. Not only is foresight important, but sharing safety concerns with children can help them learn to be careful hikers.

The trails we include in this guide are well marked or easily followed paths, but it is always possible to stray from the trail. A child who follows an interesting animal, or investigates a sight or sound, can easily leave the trail. Keeping your group together is the single best precaution against someone getting lost.

Always bring a map and trail description. Learn how to read the map and begin to pass on that knowledge as soon as your child is old enough to understand. Rocky or treeless sections of trail can be harder to follow. Cairns (heaps of stones that mark a route) or paint blazes may help, but a watchful eye for continuation of the trail is needed.

Children may enjoy leading the group rather than following the adults. This is also good practice for learning to read the trail. Stay within sight, but let them learn what to watch for. If they lose the trail and do not get back on track, help them find it again. Stress the importance of being aware of the trail.

The descent is almost always more difficult and dangerous than the ascent. Paths converge on a peak, but lines of descent radiate outward, and the wrong path can take a hiker far afield. Leaving the trail can lead to impassable cliffs or dangerously steep slopes. Especially when descending from a bare summit, be sure of your bearing and make certain that you are taking the proper trail.

Safety Tips for the Trail

SOME GENERAL SAFETY RULES ARE:

- Use the buddy system (hike in pairs)
- Wait for your entire group to reassemble at each trail junction, or at any point where the way is unclear
- Dress children in brightly colored clothes so they are easier to see
- Have each hiker, whether adult or child, carry a whistle (three blasts is the signal for help)
- Stay within calling distance of one another

If you, as group leader, have lost the trail, it is usually best to stop, try to orient yourself on the map, and retrace your route until you regain the trail. It is not wise to launch out in the direction you hope will be correct.

Be sure that children understand the following before starting on a hike:

- — if they are lost, stay where they are (hug a tree!)
- — you will not be angry with them or punish them for being lost, but will be glad when they are safely found
- — search and rescue people will be looking for them; this is one time when it is fine to talk to strangers
- — if they hear an airplane or helicopter, try to go to a clearing and wave both arms

If one or more people become lost or separated from the group, mark the last known location of the missing party on the map, to use in the event a search needs to be organized. If emergency assistance is needed, contact DEC Emergency Dispatch at 518-891-0235.

This is a 24-hour number. If they cannot be reached, call the New York State Police at 518-897-2000. If someone is sent to call for help, in the event of a medical emergency, for example, make sure the person knows the exact location of the person needing help. A location map and written message with time, place, and description of the emergency is recommended.

Other safety considerations to keep in mind when hiking with children include:

— Wet or moss-covered rocks or roots can be very slippery.

— Hiking when there is a thick cover of fallen leaves on the trail requires caution in rocky sections.

— When climbing on fallen trees, be careful of dead limbs which may easily break off.

— When crossing streams, have an adult go first to lend a hand on the other side or show the best route. Walking sticks may add stability.

— Remember that children's legs do not reach as far as yours. When the trail becomes steep, have an adult behind the child on the way up and an adult in front on the way down. In fact, descents can be more difficult. We have had more skinned knees on the way down, which was probably partly due to tired legs.

— Climbing up boulders tends to be easier than getting down from them.

— If you get caught in a storm, avoid lone or tall trees, streams, peaks, and large open flat areas. A clump of trees lower than others around it may be safe.

— Don't eat plants or berries unless you are positive of their identification. Be able to identify poison ivy and poison oak.

— Check out lunch sites or campsites and warn children of potential dangers, such as broken glass or steep drop-offs.

Hunting Seasons

Hikers should be aware that, unlike the national parks, sport hunting is permitted on all public lands and much of the private land within the Adirondack Park. There are separate regulations and seasons for each type of hunting—small game, waterfowl, and big game. It is the big game season (deer and bear) that is most likely to cause concern for hikers. The following is a list of all big game hunting seasons, which run from approximately mid-September through early December.

EARLY BEAR SEASON: Begins on the first Saturday after the second Monday in September and continues for four weeks.

ARCHERY SEASON: September 27 to opening of the regular season.

MUZZLE-LOADING SEASON: The seven days prior to the opening of the regular season.

REGULAR SEASON: Begins on the next to last Saturday in October and continues through the first Sunday in December.

During any of these open seasons, prudence dictates the wearing of at least one piece of orange, red, or other brightly colored clothing. The chance of encountering hunters on mountain trails is relatively small given that the game being pursued do not favor the steeper slopes. Be forewarned that you may encounter hunters around waterfalls, lakes, and other lowland areas.

Trail Etiquette

Hiking is so much more pleasurable when trails and the wilderness are well maintained and when hikers interact with each other in respectful ways. It's important for adults to serve as role models and to teach their children trail etiquette. The pleasure children derive from being noisy, running with boundless energy, and gathering countless objects for their collections need not be totally squelched, just directed in acceptable ways.

Quiet Time with Nature

There are aspects of wilderness that are not appreciated as much by children as by adults. Peace and quiet don't hold much attraction for our children—who seem intent all too often on abolishing them. Reminders that others may wish to be able to enjoy the gentle sounds of nature are in order. When we are the only hikers on the trail we don't worry too much about noise. When we know there are others on the trail, especially if they are quietly enjoying the views from a summit, we try not to intrude too much.

Trail Preservation

It's essential that children learn the importance of staying on the trail. Aside from reasons of safety, there are concerns over trail conditions. If erosion due to hiking can be limited to the trails, then the flora and fauna of the area will be disturbed as little as possible. It's best to avoid hiking at very wet times since the tendency to go around mud and water widens the existing trail. When you and your child begin climbing to summits that are above tree line, it's important to stay on rock as much as possible to preserve the fragile alpine vegetation, which is extremely susceptible and slow to recover from damage by foot traffic.

Gathering Along the Way

Children love to collect things. Gathering a bouquet of dandelions from the back yard is very different from gathering the lady's slippers you find on a spring woods walk. Your child may be old enough to understand the concepts of endangerment of species and fragility of balances in nature. The impact on the natural world if every person in the world were to "only pick one" can be understood by many children. The difference between picking cultivated flowers, which can be planted again, and picking from small pockets of wildflowers can be explained. The idea of "dead and down" is also a useful concept for children. Harvesting an assortment of fallen leaves or small twigs probably does little harm, whereas pulling leaves, branches, or bark from trees should be forbidden. Teach the power of getting down to observe something, and leaving it undisturbed, rather than picking it up to look at it.

If children are too young to understand these concepts, then just have a rule that they must check with you before they pick anything. Watch and direct their explorations. Many hikers go by the principle, "Take only pictures and leave only footprints." Leave things in place so others can enjoy them, too.

Children also love to throw things. Throwing a stone or stick along the trail and into the woods is probably fine, but do not let children throw objects from mountaintops or down steep sections of the trail. The greatest danger lies in children hurling themselves over a ledge as they hurl a large stone, or in striking a hiker coming up the trail from below.

Being the Leader

Many children have an obsession about being first. Our two are no different. What usually works is giving each child a certain amount of time to be the leader, but with leadership go certain responsibilities. The leader makes sure that he or she is not getting too far ahead of the others and tries to keep the pace comfortable for the slowest hiker. The leader warns the others of a particularly slippery spot or one where the footing is tricky. If there are branches extending into the trail, the leader makes sure they don't whip back to hurt the next hiker.

If You Carry It in, Carry It Out

Most children are taught that littering is wrong. That pertains to littering on hiking trails as well. When stopping for a snack or lunch, make sure to leave no sign of your presence. In fact, we also clean up litter others have left if we have a way to carry it out.

Hiking with the Family Dog

Dogs should be kept under an owner's direct control at all times. An eager and rambunctious dog running along the trail can startle a young hiker and knock him down. Restrain your dog on a leash when others approach. Clean droppings away from trail and camping areas. Note that dogs are not allowed on trails within the Adirondack Mountain Reserve, in the Ausable Lake area.

Special Considerations for Infants and Toddlers (0–2 years)

When we had children, we realized we wanted to continue hiking and that we wanted to do it with our babies. The outdoor world, its sights and sounds and smells, did not have to wait until they were independent hikers. They grew up seeing that walks in nature are one of the many things we do together.

We had to shorten distances and no longer just think of our own comfort. We carried our children around with us quite a bit. When they had developed greater neck strength, at about five or six months of age, we changed from a front carrier to a framed backpack child carrier for our evening walks, walks to town, and then for hikes. We suggest you practice by carrying the young child around the house in a carrier or backpack during everyday activities. Not only can it settle an unhappy baby, but you'll also get used to the feel of the weight and learn how to rebalance yourself. Like the legend of the old woman who could carry a huge ox, if you start when they're small, your strength will increase along with the baby's gain in weight.

We used both a small framed backpack and the larger, sturdier type with a hip belt, which was more comfortable for both adult and child. The larger packs have a small storage area for carrying diapers, wipes, and other needed items, and a higher back to support the head of a napping infant. Technology has evolved rapidly, making carrying infants quite pleasant for both adult and baby.

Diapering needs to be considered. Always bring more diapers than you think you will need. It's not too difficult to plan for day trips. We carried a bag with the diapers, a small pad on which to lay the child, and something to wipe up messes. You also will need to carry a plastic bag in which to place soiled diapers. Never bury, burn, or leave diapers along the trail or in the woods. If you are planning to camp in the wilderness, Cindy Ross and Todd Gladfelter's book, *Kids in the Wild*, (Mountaineer, 1995) provides advice on using cloth diapers in the backcountry and other tips for successful camping with infants.

When you are carrying infants for the whole hike, you set the pace. Once you know how long your child stays happy in a backpack, you can plan distances accordingly. Take frequent rests, both for yourself and to give the infant some time out of the pack. Nursing breaks make good rest times.

Make sure children drink plenty of liquids, especially if the weather is warm. Easy-to-eat finger foods are good hiking snacks.

Special Considerations for Young Children (2–5 years)

As children become confident on their own two feet, they are no longer willing to be carried in a backpack for the whole trip. Hiking expectations and goals must change once again. We no longer planned long treks into the backcountry. We were content with exploring smaller places with our children, and these turned out to be just as spectacular and rewarding. Once in a while we desired a "big" trip. That's when grandparents or friends came in handy to watch the children while we went off for the day. Sometimes one of us hiked with friends while the other parent spent the day with the children.

With young children, it's very important that new experiences be positive. We hiked only on nice days, kept our goals small until we knew our children's capabilities, and enjoyed our forays into nature.

Best Bets for Two- to Five-Year-Old Hikers

North-Northwest Section
Coon Mountain
Silver Lake Bog

**Tupper Lake, Cranberry Lake,
& Northwest Section**
Bear Mountain
Bear Mountain Bog
Fernow Forest Self-Guided Nature Trail
Floodwood Mountain
Lampson Falls and Grass River Trail
Mt. Arab
Panther Mountain
Stone Valley Trails

**Lake Placid, Saranac Lake,
& Paul Smiths Section**
Brewster Peninsula Nature Trails
Mt. Jo
Owen and Copperas Ponds
Red Dot Trail
Visitor Interpretive Center at Paul Smiths

Keene, Keene Valley Section
Baxter Mountain
Big Crow Mountain
Gulf Brook Lean-to and Lost Pond
Owls Head (Keene)

Minerva, Newcomb Section
Boreas River Trail
Visitor Interpretive Center at Newcomb

**Old Forge, Long Lake,
& Blue Mountain Section**
Rocky Mountain

Indian Lake & South Section
Auger Falls

Children of this age have an agenda that is very different from that of adults. The idea of reaching a destination is seldom the reason for the hike. Concepts of time and distance are vague. The idea that a mile-long hike should take an hour doesn't mean much to three- or four-year-olds. They are entertained by the events, objects, and moods of the moment. If there's a little stream to explore, a neat rock to observe, or a colorful leaf to catch the eye, they will stop. Allow lots of time for a hike when you are encouraging your young hikers to do some or most of the walking. You will achieve a new understanding of the natural world when you try to explain objects and events to your children in a way they will understand. "How do trees grow around a huge rock?" "Why can a tree grow on a rock?" "Why is there a pile of pinecone pieces here?" This stage of "low key" hiking doesn't last forever, so enjoy it for what it is.

Select your child's high-energy part of the day to hike, if at all possible. For many children, the early part of the day is best, before they've expended energy in other ways.

You should still expect to be carrying younger children much of the time. At this age they may only hike a half-mile per hour. They may be in and out of the backpack, or going piggyback, or up on your shoulders now and then. Don't make them feel that being carried means they're giving up. Young children get tired much more quickly than adults do. Hiking conditions or your child's mood and energy level will be just right one day and she'll experience her first "unassisted" hike. It's a very proud moment for a young hiker, so go ahead and make a big deal about it.

Some of our best hiking experiences were when other children joined the party. They entertained each other and stamina and good behavior seemed to be in more plentiful supply. Older friends (those seven- to ten-year-olds who like to help out the younger ones) are great role models. Our oldest son did his first unaided hike (almost four miles round-trip) when he was three. He had an energetic seven-year-old buddy who made it fun and painless. When considering companions for the trail, it's a good idea to discuss everyone's expectations. Are all willing to hike at the pace of the slowest hiker?

Children need minigoals. "It's not too far until we cross the brook," or "We'll be getting to a steep part with boulders soon." Young kids seem to like rugged climbing more than long, flat stretches. The top of a mountain does not always have to be a goal for the very young, but the four- and five-year-olds may be motivated by getting to the top. To help young children envision distances more concretely, it helps to talk of the distance still to cover in familiar terms, such as "It's only as far as our walk to the library, and we'll be at the top!"

We never expected our children to carry gear when they were younger. We wanted their first experiences to be unencumbered and as enjoyable as possible. Some parents may want their children to share in the work of the hike. We felt that there were plenty of hikes ahead of them when they'd be stronger and ready to help shoulder the day packs. On the other hand, some children may want to carry a pack so that they feel they are really hiking. One young friend wanted his pack, which contained a small water bottle and magnifier. As long as what they want to carry along is reasonable, don't discourage it, but realize you may eventually be shouldering the extra pack.

Special Considerations for Older Children (6–12 years)

Parents may find children of this age to be the most satisfying hiking companions. Physically they can be quite capable hikers, and they still like being with their parents. At this age our children rarely slowed us down. In fact, often they were happily setting the pace ahead of us. This is when children's confidence in their hiking skills develops. They can accept more distant goals, so longer hikes are possible. They can also do a larger share of trip planning and preparation.

Children of this age can be quite able day hikers. We still did not expect our children to carry any gear for the day outings. This meant they hiked more freely and made it a more enjoyable experience for them. They were able to cover more miles without a pack if we attempted a longer or more challenging hike. Children expend more energy lifting their legs higher over boulders and taking more steps with their shorter strides.

We let our children take turns as trip leader. Being the leader for a set amount of time worked well. We still used "power pill" candies at this age when energy ran low, but they usually were an indication that a rest or food and water stop was needed. "Power pills" became more of an enticement for them to wait for us. "If you wait at that big rock up there, I'll pull out those power pills!" Our long-term endurance was still greater than theirs, but their short bursts of energy could easily surpass ours.

Some children don't like being last on the trail. Others find it frightening. Don't force them to take that position if it makes them uncomfortable. An adult who can survey the situation can best bring up the rear. Other children may be reluctant hikers. See if a reason can be found. It may be something as simple as needing more rest time or a snack or drink. Maybe you've overestimated the child's abilities. Never send a child back to the car or trailhead alone. If more than one adult is on the hike and the child cannot be convinced to continue, have an adult accompany the child. If not, all need to end the hike.

As children become more confident hikers, they begin to have greater expectations for themselves. "I can get across that stream without any help." "I can scramble up these boulders myself." "I'm ready for the highest mountain now!" Allow them to test limits safely or begin to offer them more challenges.

Many children of this age are fascinated with maps. Let children look at the road atlas or map in the car as you drive to the trailhead. Look at the trail map with them before starting the hike. Children may even begin to use a compass by comparing compass bearings with trail orientation on the map. Few trails are straight lines, and major bends can often be identified with map and compass. Next comes the ability to understand contour lines on topographic maps. Reading the guidebook descriptions can lead to practice estimating trail position. The subtleties of compass-reading can come later, but the fundamentals are easily learned.

At some point children will realize that status accrues from doing "big name" peaks. They will probably discover this before they have the strength and stamina to enjoy these more rigorous climbs. The High Peaks really have no more, and often less, intrinsic interest than the lower summits we include in this guide. If the desire to do the big ones cannot be resisted, High Peaks trips can be reserved as prizes for the proven hiker. Mt. Marcy is on our agenda—it's something of a holy grail for the Adirondack hiker.

Will the time come when our children no longer want to hike with us? That may depend on our relationship with them and on how much of their time is absorbed by other interests. Perhaps they will be interested in new challenges, such as longer excursions, winter adventures, or more rigorous climbs. Maybe they'll leave hiking for a while and return to it later. We hope that their time spent in the natural world will influence their future perspectives.

Camping

Backpacking into the wilderness is not our focus in this book, but we do want to discuss special considerations for wilderness camping with children.

The right time to begin wilderness camping with children depends on many factors, the most important being that you, the adult, feel capable and knowledgeable about wilderness camping. The amount of energy you are willing to expend and the tolerance you have for the extra work involved in keeping a toddler safe and occupied while you tend to other matters is a personal decision.

Friends of ours decided to try a car camping adventure with a thirteen-month-old who had just started walking and a five-year-old. They found the work involved in keeping the younger child out of harm's way left the burden of camp details primarily to the other parent. Their experience was not an enjoyable one. They did not give up on the idea, but realized that camping would be easier when the baby is a little older. The father planned some camping overnights with just his five-year-old son. It gave them some time alone and the older boy began learning new skills. Other families take on the challenge of camping with toddlers and do fine. Each family is different.

Overnight camping with infants, when you are not car camping, takes much preparation. Consider all the gear you need for two adults without an infant. If one person is carrying an infant, packing all of your gear will need to be done very carefully. If the experience proves stressful and too difficult, it may best be put off until your children are no longer infants or toddlers. We did some canoe camping when we had only one child, but most of our other camping experiences were limited to car camping when both boys were very young.

Our first wilderness camping experience with both boys was when they had just turned two and four. We knew they could not carry all the extra gear we would need, so our first few trips were with the help of their uncle. Three adults seemed to be able to meet the needs of all. By the time the boys were four and six, they were able to carry small school backpacks. Since we all shared one tent, we were able to carry all that was needed for two adults and two children.

When the boys were six and eight we began to do much more wilderness camping. At first we chose places that did not involve long hikes into the campsite. There are many campsites that are away from main thoroughfares but are only one-half mile to two miles walk. Many times we hiked in one place and drove to another trailhead to hike into our planned camping spot. As you gain experience in wilderness camping with your children and know your capabilities, you can cover longer distances.

Backpacks

On our first few camping trips, which were very short, the kids simply carried their school backpacks, each with a sleeping bag and a change of clothing. Once the children weighed 55–60 lbs (25-27kg), they seemed to be ready for a child-sized frame pack (available at larger outdoor recreation stores or through mail order catalogs). As with adults, frame packs make carrying a load much easier by distributing some of the weight to the hips. We felt the investment was worth it because they would get many years use out of them and the packs could be resold or passed on to other beginning hikers.

Our boys were very excited the day their backpacks arrived. They wore them around the house. We packed them up for practice. Our first time out with the packs was a very short walk from the car to a campsite. The next night we had a longer hike to our campsite and we made sure to select a level trail. The boys had to adjust to the way the packs changed their sense of balance, especially when they bent over, and to the fact that the packs slowed them down a bit.

Their packs don't have a very large capacity and we don't want them to be too heavy. They typically carry:

— sleeping bag inside the pack
— sleeping pad attached to the outside (once we began to need a second tent, one boy carried both pads and the other carried the tent)
— rain gear and a change of clothes (especially socks)
— a wool sweater or polar fleece jacket
— a water bottle
— a book or journal and pencil
— slippers or slip-on shoes for the campsite
— a favorite stuffed animal or two, hanging out of the small front pocket

We packed books and clothing in plastic just in case we were caught in the rain.

Tents, Sleeping Bags, and Pads

We like to stay in lean-tos, and usually can, but we always carry a tent (two tents now that the kids are bigger) just in case. Early in the season, bugs can be such a problem that the insect-proof tent is much preferred. Late in the season, the tent can be warmer than a windy lean-to. A popular spot on a busy weekend can also mean full lean-tos and no choice but to pitch a tent. It is usually possible to find established tent spots in the vicinity of lean-tos. Remember to abide by regulations for setback from trails and water. There is no camping allowed within 150 ft. (46 m) of a stream, other water source, or trail, except at designated campsites. Most areas near lean-tos are considered designated campsites.

Occasionally we have camped in state parks and felt dwarfed by (and a bit envious of) the lofty, roomy tents erected by our neighboring campers. Our roomy two-person tent, which served us well when our two children were quite small, is designed to be light (8 lb. [4 kg]) rather than to accommodate lawn chairs. It's a squeeze, but the low profile and dome design have advantages other than low weight. It can be pitched in a relatively small area, and will withstand winds that may damage or destroy "family-camping" style tents.

If your children have not had any experience in a tent, it's a good idea to begin in the backyard or by car camping. The more often you camp, the better and easier the preparation becomes. You learn to anticipate what you will need and what will keep everyone happy, safe, and comfortable. The children adjust to the idea of having just a piece of plastic between them and the night and with the feeling of sleeping on the ground. Our children looked forward to an excuse to sleep outside.

Now we have a second, smaller tent for the kids. It's actually a roomy one-person tent and very light (3½ lb. [1.6 kg]). The boys fit very well inside and they love having their own "house."

Child-sized sleeping bags are available in a variety of qualities and prices. In cooler weather, a smaller sleeping bag that fits well will keep a child warmer. A nylon and synthetic fill bag has advantages over cotton, in that it is lighter weight and performs better if damp. Down-filled sleeping bags are warm, but not effective when wet. It should not be necessary to spend a lot of money on a sleeping bag that will only be used in mild weather. A cotton or synthetic sleeping bag liner will make it easier to keep sleeping bags clean and may be all that is needed on warm summer nights. If you contemplate winter camping, seek the advice of a good camping equipment supplier.

Our experience is that children can sleep on almost any dry flat surface, no matter how hard. Even so, we carry thin foam pads for them (they are essential for adult hikers). In cooler conditions, the insulating value of the pad is important for everyone's comfortable rest. Pillows can be improvised from extra clothing.

Most other aspects of successful camping—site selection, cooking, cleanup, sanitation—are not materially different because of the presence of children. There is much information available that will help make for a good camping experience. Many sources offer advice on equipment, recipes, and general technique and planning (see Selected References).

Wildlife

Large wildlife is not particularly abundant in the Adirondacks, and probably never has been. Some of the larger carnivores have been extirpated, or nearly so, including the wolf, mountain lion, lynx, and bobcat. Controversy continues over proposals to reintroduce these species. The deer population, however, is thought to be greater now than it was a hundred or more years ago.

Bears remain the largest wild animals in the Park (apart from a few reported moose), but even they are seldom seen in most areas. Nonetheless, campers should always hang food out of reach of all wildlife, the possible bear included. Numerous smaller mammals are abundant, including beaver (now very common following their near disappearance in the early 1800s), muskrats, rabbits, raccoons, squirrels, porcupines, and weasels. All are elusive.

Some animals may be heard far more easily than they are seen. Coyote, estimated by the DEC to number 18,000 in northern New York in 1991, may sometimes be heard howling at night. Some of the birds of the deep forest are heard far more often than seen.

Beaver are fairly common, best caught at their work in early morning or evening. Deer are certainly the most ubiquitous large animal, but no less exciting to children for their prevalence. In the village of Old Forge, deer are so numerous and bold as to have become a nuisance. An interesting history of man's relationship with mammals in the Adirondacks can be found in *Wildlife and Wilderness: A History of Adirondack Mammals*, by Philip G. Terrie.

Sighting wildlife, especially these creatures not common in developed areas, can be the highlight of a hike. Since such events are unpredictable and rare, it is best not to raise expectations. Let the lucky encounter come as a true surprise, as seeing beaver kits scrambling over a dam on the trail to Jenkins Mountain was for us. Discourage any child's attempts to feed wild animals, and be alert to the danger of rabies.

We have more often been delighted to spy the smaller, less reclusive, creatures. Toads, salamanders, newts, songbirds, insects, the occasional snake—these can be seen on almost any hike, and are also wonderful.

Hiking and the Seasons

Each season in the Adirondacks has its own attractions and each has some disadvantages. It's wise to know what to expect when taking children on the trail.

Spring

Spring can come late in the Adirondacks. It is not unusual to encounter surprisingly deep snow as you climb up from flower-covered lower elevations. Walks along rivers and waterfalls can be especially impressive when the flows are at their peak. Along with spring flowers, you can expect muddy trails often. Be aware of the harm you may be causing to soft trails. Steep trails, especially those already showing the effects of erosion, should be avoided.

A good guidebook to local wildflower species is fun to have at this time of year. Children quickly come to know trillium, pink lady's slipper, trout lily, and bunchberry. Teach them to get low and observe or even to sketch or photograph if they are so inclined, but not to pick.

Summer

Summer is really two seasons in the Adirondacks. Early summer is blackfly season. When this season begins and ends is variable, in terms of both time and location. When the bugs are out at low elevations, the upper slopes may still be pest-free. Head nets with mesh fine enough to keep out the tiny but vicious blackflies are our preferred defense. When it gets bad enough for nets, it may be best to wait for conditions to improve. It is almost impossible for anyone, and especially children, to appreciate a hike while fighting a war with blackflies. Within a few weeks blackflies have usually disappeared and mosquitoes are the main insect pest. They can be dealt with in the same way. Even at their worst, mosquito problems vary greatly from place to place. A breezy spot can be relatively mosquito-free, while a spot near a breeding ground and without air movement can have swarms. Hot, dry weather in midsummer usually means the end of significant discomfort from insects.

The long summer days are ideal for a camping trip or a long hike. At the end of July and August we keep a lookout for blueberries on the summits or other open sunny spots. We often carry an extra plastic container with us or use an emptied water bottle for berries. Make sure very young children check with you before eating anything on the trail. Other berries also grow low to the ground. An adult may know it's not a blueberry, but it may not be so obvious to a child.

Fall

Fall is in most respects the best time for hiking in the Adirondacks. Bothersome bugs are minimal, days are not too hot, nights are cool but not frigid. Add the glories of fall foliage, and it is easy to understand why the trails are at their busiest on autumn weekends. Only the decreasing hours of daylight and the likelihood of finding lean-tos occupied on weekends can be held against this season. If you can hike on weekdays, all the better, but don't miss fall in the mountains. Remember that fall is hunting season, though, so dress in bright colors.

Our favorite plant to spot in early fall is jewelweed, also known as touch-me-nots. As the pretty orange flowers pass away, we look for plump seedpods that burst open at the slightest touch. Mushrooms, especially plentiful after wet spells in late summer and fall, can also be great fun to spot and try to identify.

Winter

Winter hiking in the Adirondacks is a serious and potentially risky undertaking. Greater exertion is required, weather changes can be abrupt and threatening, and the presence of children on a winter outing makes any misadventures more complex. Even when properly dressed, hypothermia and frostbite are possible hazards. Prepare yourself well by learning about safe outdoor practices in this most dangerous season. Winter outings require cross-country skis or snowshoes, as walking in deep snow is very difficult, if not impossible. If your children are comfortable on skis or snowshoes, winter excursions can be beautiful. The one thing we always keep in mind is that our children exert much more energy than we do in skiing or snowshoeing and their pace is much slower. It's very important for adults to dress warmly, as they will not be generating much heat when they are moving at children's slower pace.

A trail hiked in one season can offer new delights in another. Revisiting places in the Adirondacks sharpens your senses to seasonal changes.

What's So Special about the Adirondacks?

Mountains, forests, and water; these three elements play a central role in the imaginative lives of most children. They are deeply embedded in our heritage as humans. Folklore, legends, and fairy tales give evidence of their universal appeal. How much of our culture would we fail to appreciate if we could not vividly imagine the presence and force of these primeval elements?

The Adirondack Mountains combine these elements in classic proportions, from the most intimate to the grand. Small peaks that can be reached on an easy walk mingle with summits and cliffs that challenge strong hikers. Well-marked trails through labeled and tamed forest are down the road from forests that bear scant evidence of the intrusion of humans. Numberless small streams and ponds feed the great lakes and rivers which flow down from the Adirondacks in all directions.

All this lies within easy reach of millions of people living in the eastern United States and Canada. The combination of public and private lands that make up the six million acres of the Adirondack Park, and the Park's relative freedom from intense development, have allowed this wonderful mix of features to survive for us to enjoy. Hikers should be aware that trails may follow rights of way permitted by landowners; thus we must respect owners' rights and abide by the conditions of use.

People who have come to know the Park's wild places, including long-time residents, value the Park for its unique qualities, but its continued survival can never be taken for granted. Even this great area could succumb to the forces that have overrun so much of our land. There is reason to hope it will not. Awareness of the importance of preserving the Adirondacks led to the creation of the Park more than 100 years ago and has been reaffirmed in subsequent generations. We hope our children will continue this tradition. Each passing year only makes more clear the wisdom of this commitment.

North–Northeast Section

The main travel arteries in this region are NY 30 running north from Paul Smiths, and NY 3 heading northeast from Saranac Lake. Rivers and lakes are as much a focus of attention as the mountains, with Lake Champlain a large presence along the eastern border.

OTHER ATTRACTIONS IN THIS SECTION :

- Almanzo Wilder Homestead, just east of Malone; the original home of "Farmer Boy" of the Laura Ingalls Wilder Little House books (518-483-1207)
- Arts Council for the Northern Adirondacks, Westport; publishes a summer events calendar (518-962-8778)
- Crown Point Historical Site, on the western shore of the Lake Champlain Bridge in Crown Point; site of a colonial fort (518-597-3666)
- Essex County Fish Hatchery, Crown Point (518-597-3844)
- 1812 Homestead, Willsboro; an early farm complex (518-963-4071)
- Ausable Chasm, near Keeseville; commercial guided tours and boat ride of the deep gorge (518-834-7454)
- Public Campgrounds (call 1-800-456-2267 for reservations)
  Ausable Point—US 9, south of Plattsburgh
  Crown Point Reservation—NY 9N, north of Crown Point
  Cumberland Bay—north of Plattsburgh
  Poke-O-Moonshine—Rt. 9 north of Elizabethtown
  Paradox Lake—north of Schroon Lake Village

1. Everton Falls

Round-trip loop: 1.2 mi. (1.9 km)
Elevation change: Minimal
Map: Santa Clara 7.5'

This Nature Conservancy property includes attractive falls on the East Branch of the St. Regis River. Below the falls there is a short loop trail through interesting forest and undergrowth. An interpretive brochure may be found at the trail entrance or obtained from the Nature Conservancy (see address in Sources appendix).

Trailhead: The falls themselves are easily seen from the Red Tavern Road, also known as County Rt. 26, 8.0 mi. (12.8 km) west from NY 30 or 7.0 mi. (11.2 km) east of its western end in St. Regis Falls. This 0.7-mi. (1.1-km) loop trail, called Balsam Trail and marked with a post, begins 0.4 mi. (0.6 km) west (downstream) of the parking pull-off by the falls on the left. This trail should not be used in April.

The main attraction of this hike is found in the abundant and diverse vegetation. Late spring is an ideal time for flowers at Everton Falls. You may wish to bring along a selection of guidebooks (wildflowers, birds, ferns, mushrooms) or a small sketch pad if your children enjoy drawing. Mosquito netting is also a good idea. The marked trail winds through a rich flat land, and is indistinct in places, but easy enough to follow. Walk at a leisurely pace, then enjoy a rest back at the falls. If you are lucky, there may be cedar waxwings hawking insects above the pool at the base of the falls. The canoe trip upstream from the falls is one of the most pleasant in the Park.

2. Silver Lake Bog
Round-trip: 2.5 mi. (4.0 km)
Elevation change: Minimal
Map: Alder Brook 7.5'

The Adirondack Nature Conservancy has constructed a 0.5-mi. (0.8-km) boardwalk through their 61-acre property near Hawkeye. An interpretive guide to the bog and woods trail (available at the register) makes this walk an excellent way to learn about several Adirondack habitats. The trail ends at bluffs overlooking Silver Lake—it's a nice spot to rest and picnic. This is an easy walk with lots to see for its length.

Trailhead: From Ausable Forks travel northwest toward Silver Lake and the hamlet of Hawkeye. Continue to the intersection with Silver Lake Road, which is coming from the north. Go straight on what is now called Union Falls Road for 1.0 mi. (1.6 km). Turn left on the Old Hawkeye Road, a poorly marked dirt road. At 0.2 mi. (0.3 km) the parking area is on the right, with a sign saying Silver Lake Camp Preserve.

The trail descends gradually from the parking area and very soon reaches the boardwalk. Notice the abrupt change in vegetation as the trail leaves dry ground and enters the bog. Fifteen stations, some with benches, highlight some of the typical features of bogs. Pitcher plants, Labrador tea, a variety of ferns, mountain holly, and other bog plants are found here, as well as a beautiful carpet of sphagnum moss. If you're lucky, you may also spot black-backed and three-toed woodpeckers.

At the end of the boardwalk, the trail continues for 0.8 mi. (1.3 km) as a marked path through mixed hardwoods. The change from bog to hardwoods trail is dramatic. Near the end the trail climbs 200 ft. (61 m) before reaching rock ledges that afford views of Silver Lake.

There's something magical about being in this place. A bog environment is not typically one to which we have access and thus it's different from anything else we usually hike. To be there in the middle of it, yet know you're not having an adverse impact on it, is special.

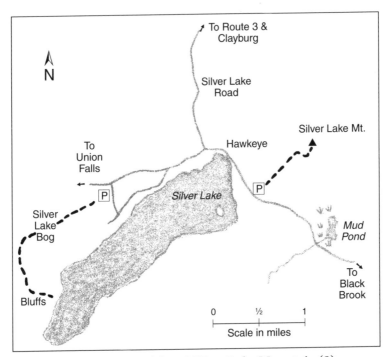

Silver Lake Bog (2) and Silver Lake Mountain (3)

3. Silver Lake Mountain

Round-trip: 1.8 mi. (2.9 km)
Elevation change: 900 ft. (274 m)
Map: Redford 7.5'

Though this hike is short, it provides a steady ascent and good views from open rock ledges along the way and at the top. (See map, p. 53.) The hike can be extended by following the long ridge along the peak, which has fine lookouts.

Trailhead: From the hamlet of Clayburg on NY 3 turn south onto Silver Lake Road. The road comes to a T-intersection in about 6.0 mi. (9.6 km) in Hawkeye. Turn left and drive to a parking area on the north side of the road 0.8 mi. (1.3 km) east of the campground on Silver Lake. The trailhead begins at the parking area.

Climbing begins almost at once through beech and maple woods with occasional ash and oak trees. Look for their numerous seedlings growing along the trail. They are easily identified by the different leaf shapes, and close enough to the ground for convenient inspection.

At 0.5 mi. (0.8 km) there is a lookout on the left. Red pine predominates as you ascend. In season, blueberries abound along this section. At 0.7 mi. (1.1 km) the trail turns sharply right and climbs around some large rocks. This turn could be missed but for the presence of two large, angular boulders immediately ahead. It may be tempting to scramble ahead past these boulders (the obvious paths prove many others have), but it is a better route to the top if you keep to the trail.

Just 0.2 mi. (0.3 km) from this turn, having crossed open rock slopes, you will arrive at the summit outcrop, with good views to Silver Lake and Taylor Pond. Catamount is beyond them and Whiteface one ridge farther off. Looking southeast you can see Mud Pond, a small lake that illustrates very well the gradual transformation of small bodies of water to wetlands, and eventually to dry land. Only a small area of open water remains, surrounded by vegetation encroaching from the shore. The summit of Silver Lake Mountain is a long ridge. A faint path continues along the ridge offering a longer walk and additional views.

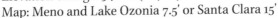

4. Azure Mountain

Round-trip: 2.0 mi. (3.2 km)
Elevation change: 940 ft. (287 m)
Map: Meno and Lake Ozonia 7.5' or Santa Clara 15'

Azure Mountain is an isolated peak in the far northern Adirondacks, with views from its bare summit of lakes and hills rumpling away on all sides. It's a steep climb for much of the way, but short.

Trailhead: Turn south on the Blue Mountain Road from NY 458, 3.0 mi. (4.8 km) north of the hamlet of Santa Clara. Drive 7.0 mi. (11.2 km) until a dirt road enters on the right, near the top of a rise, and just past a marked spring. It may be possible to drive 0.1 mi. (0.2 km) down the road to a small parking area, if conditions are not too wet.

The trail starts at a gate, and proceeds along the road 0.3 mi. (0.5 km) to the site of a former observer's cabin. The red-marked trail continues, becoming more steep. Recent rerouting of the trail directs hikers away from the steep and badly eroded herd path that follows the old telephone line directly up the mountain. Staying on the marked trail makes a more pleasant walk, and will help vegetation become reestablished in the eroded areas.

At 0.9 mi. (1.4 km) the trail moderates. Some low cliffs appear on the right, and the summit is at hand. The final 0.1 mi. (0.2 km) leads through tall grass to the fire tower (the stairs are removed to prevent climbing) and open rock. The cliffs on the south side, popular with local technical rock climbers, provide splendid views, and have also been used as hacking sites in efforts to reintroduce falcons to the area. The summit of St. Regis Mountain is easily seen to the south. Looking northwest, one can see the length of Lake Ozonia. It is quite common to see hawks and ravens soaring overhead, or in the valley below this wild and remote peak.

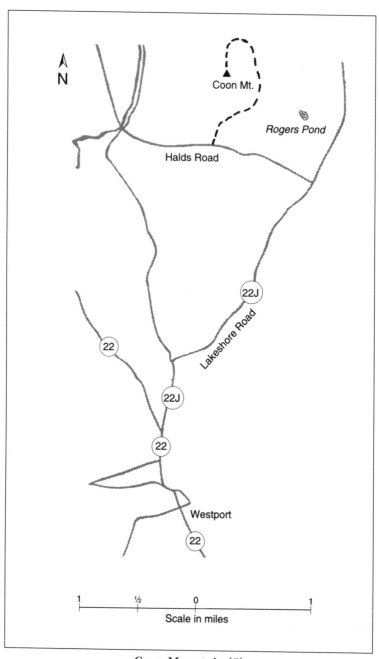

N

Coon Mt.

Rogers Pond

Halds Road

22J

Lakeshore Road

22

22J

22

Westport

22

1   ½   0   1
Scale in miles

Coon Mountain (5)

5. Coon Mountain

Round-trip: 2.0 mi. (3.2 km)
Elevation change: 500 ft. (152 m)
Map: Westport 7.5', Port Henry 15', or Westport metric

This trail was a very pleasant surprise. A short but occasionally steep trail winds around and up little Coon Mountain, just north of Westport. The upper slopes of Coon Mountain have been protected as part of the Adirondack Land Trust's 246-acre preserve. This is a great hike for the beginner. The 500 ft. (152 m) of climbing, mostly done in a few very steep sections, will leave no doubt that a mountain has been topped, but the round-trip distance is only 2.0 mi. (3.2 km).

Trailhead: Going north on NY 22 out of Westport, turn right onto Lakeshore Road at 0.4 mi. (0.6 km). After about 3.0 mi. (4.8 km), turn left onto Halds Road (no sign). The marked entrance to the parking area for the trailhead is on the right within a mile.

Easy walking at first gives way to some steeper patches. Soon the imposing gray cliffs of Coon Mountain can be spotted through the trees. A very steep stretch leads past these walls. Climbing is greatly facilitated by stones, placed as steps most of the way. Care should be taken on some larger slanted rocks; they can be quite slippery. At one point the trail comes directly to a large rock face. To the left a short path leads to a lookout; the main trail continues along the base of the wall to the right. The top is mainly open, with fine views of farms and the eastern range of the Adirondacks. To the south one sees Westport Bay on Lake Champlain. Split Rock Mountain dominates the view to the east.

Pools develop in low areas in the spring, providing breeding grounds for both frogs and salamanders along this trail. Female spotted newts, yellow-brown or green with black peppered markings, lay eggs on water plants in late winter and early spring. The bright orange young leave the water as efts in the fall and live on land for up to three years. Patches of jewelweed (or touch-me-nots) are also along the trail. They have bright orange flowers in the summer and provide seedpods whose contents spring at you when touched in the fall. Blueberries abound on the summit in late July and August.

6. Owls Head Mountain

Round-trip: 2.2 mi. (3.5 km)
Elevation change: 700 ft. (213 m)
Map: Owls Head 7.5'

It's not often that you get as good a look at the objective of a hike as you do on this one. From the shoulder of the road you can look right up at the cliffs where you will soon be eating your picnic lunch. This peak is at the northern border of the park, and offers fine views of the lakes and peaks of the northern Adirondacks.

Trailhead: On NY 30, about 12.0 mi. (19.2 km) south of Malone or about 8.0 mi. (12.8 km) north of the intersection with NY 458, go east on County Rt. 26 (formerly Rt. 99). In 4.2 mi. (6.7 km) the continuation of Rt. 26 turns right. Stay straight, heading for Mountain View. From that hamlet continue on County Rt. 27 to the main intersection in the hamlet of Owls Head. Turn right and drive under the power lines, making the next left. You will see Owls Head Mountain on your right. Park on the shoulder of the road, taking care not to obstruct the driveway.

Begin walking under the power lines. Just past the second set of poles the trail turns right through brush and small trees and crosses a blueberry field. It meets an old road and turns left (watch for this junction on your return; it's harder to spot from this direction). The walking is flat along here. In a few hundred yards the trail turns left, away from the road. The woods are thick balsam fir here, with green paint blazes to mark the way. After crossing an old corduroy road, the trail begins to climb gently. Steeper climbing begins at 0.4 mi. (0.6 km) up an eroded wash.

The trail begins to traverse the side of the mountain, bearing south. At 0.8 mi. (1.3 km) an indistinct junction is reached, with the main trail turning left and steeply upward. If you continue straight ahead at the junction, a short path leads to an abandoned mine. Magnetite had been mined here, but other minerals may be found in the tailings below the mine. Brown sunstone, a form of feldspar that reflects light, is the most interesting.

From the mine return to the junction and the main trail. It is only a few hundred yards to the summit from here, but it is the steepest part of the hike. The best views are from the top of the cliffs on the south side of the peak. Lyon Mountain is to the east, the high peaks to the south far off, with Debar Mountain near at hand to the south-southwest.

We once had a large number of families along for this outing. The companionship was nice but we learned a few lessons about hiking with a group. The larger the group, the harder it is to stay together. People have their own pace, stop for different needs, and expect different things from a hike. We thought everyone was ready and we started down the trail. One woman with an infant had decided to make a last minute diaper change. She started a few minutes later and missed the first right-hand turn onto the trail. She eventually found us, but only after much frustration. When a group is large, each smaller unit should have a trail description and map. With large groups, it is important to have a knowledgeable trail sweep.

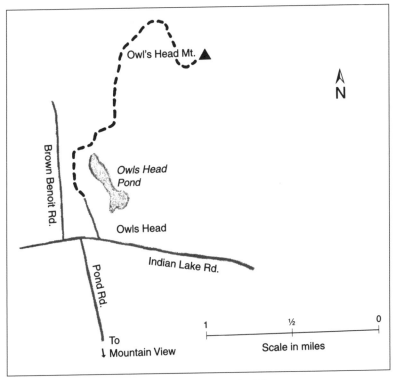

Owls Head Mountain (6)

7. Poke-O-Moonshine

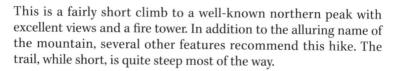

Round-trip: 2.4 mi. (3.8 km)
Elevation change: 1280 ft. (390 m)
Map: Clintonville 7.5', Ausable Forks 15', or Ausable Forks metric

This is a fairly short climb to a well-known northern peak with excellent views and a fire tower. In addition to the alluring name of the mountain, several other features recommend this hike. The trail, while short, is quite steep most of the way.

Trailhead: The trail starts at the state campground on NY 9, 9.3 mi. (14.9 km) north of the junction of the road from Lewis to Exit 32 on the Adirondack Northway and 3.0 mi. (4.8 km) south of Exit 33. There is a parking fee charged at the campground and parking on the highway in front of the campground is prohibited. Hikers should either be prepared to pay the fee or to walk a few hundred yards down the road from the "no parking" zone.

Shortly into the hike, at 0.3 mi. (0.5 km), the trail arrives at the base of immense cliffs. Rock falls have produced "caves" of considerable size. Your children might enjoy spending some time here. The trail turns left and reaches a good lookout at 0.4 mi. (0.6 km). At 0.8 mi. (1.3 km) the trail reaches a saddle with the remains of the fire observer's cabin. This is a picturesque spot and a nice place for a rest. From here the trail climbs and approaches the summit from the west. Two trails lead to the top. The left trail, now the official route, leads past a lookout before turning right and up to the summit. The right trail going up to the peak from the cabin is badly eroded and should be avoided. Summit views of Lake Champlain to the east and the high peaks to the south are superb. The fire tower has received extensive renovation (2000) from a local volunteer group in cooperation with the DEC. On clear days peaks in the Green Mountains of Vermont, including Mansfield and Camel's Hump, and even Mount Royal in far off Montreal, may be visible.

8. Debar Mountain

Round-trip: 7.4 mi. (11.8 km)
Elevation change: 1726 ft. (221 m)
Map: Meacham Lake and Debar Mt. 7.5'; or Santa Clara 15'

This is a longer hike through open woods with a steep scramble at the end. Children should have some hiking experience. They will need stamina for the final push to the top, but the views from this relatively isolated northern peak are worth the climb. This is also possible as a camping trip. A lean-to is located in the notch just below the final pitch.

Trailhead: Access is from the DEC campground and day-use area on Meacham Lake (small fee for day-use). The campground is off NY 30, 9.5 mi. (15.2 km) north of Paul Smiths. Take the DEC campsite road on the right to the campground entrance. A dirt road leads west from campsite 48 to the trailhead and a parking area in an old gravel pit. If in doubt, ask for directions at the entrance gate.

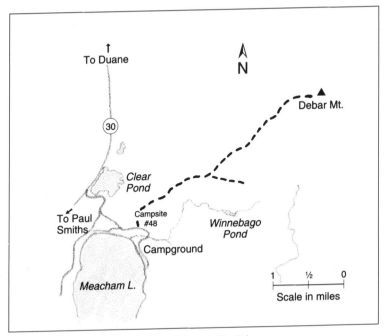

Debar Mountain (8)

The trail starts on a dirt road that is barricaded to vehicles. There is an intersection at 0.3 mi. (0.5 km); the trail stays to the right. At 0.7 mi. (1.1 km) the trail, still quite flat, passes through spruce. The trail crosses a small stream at 1.0 mi. (1.6 km). At 1.1 mi. (1.8 km) the trail to Debar Mountain branches left, indicated by red DEC markers. Open hardwoods (birch, maple, and beech) line the moderately rising trail at this point. At 2.0 mi. (3.2 km) the trail reaches a high point, levels off, then drops a bit. It climbs to a lean-to below the peak of Debar Mountain at 2.9 mi. (4.6 km). Just beyond is an overgrown field and the foundation of the former fire observer's cabin. This is a good spot to take a rest and have a snack to prepare for the climb ahead. Almost immediately the trail gets steep, with some very challenging spots, and a good deal of rock scrambling. At 3.7 mi. (5.9 km) the trail reaches the bare rocks of the summit. Views to the west are exceptional, with hills rolling off seemingly endlessly. Meacham Lake is prominent to the southwest.

Allow plenty of time on the summit for everyone to rest. The first part of the descent requires extra caution because it is so steep. It is still a long walk from the lean-to back to the trailhead, but the trail is easy to follow and a gradual descent from that point. Rewards are definitely in order following this hike. If the season and weather are right, the beach at Meacham Lake is quite attractive.

9. Catamount

Round-trip: 3.6 mi. (5.8 km)
Elevation change: 1542 ft. (470 m)
Map: Wilmington 7.5′ and Franklin Falls 7.5′, Lake Placid 15′, or Wilmington metric

Catamount is probably one of the most spectacular small peaks in the Adirondacks. Experienced rock scramblers will enjoy this trip, but it is not a hike for beginners or very young children.

Trailhead: The trailhead is not well-marked. From NY 86 in the center of Wilmington, follow the Whiteface Memorial Highway for 2.8 mi. (4.5 km) and turn right onto the Franklin Falls Road. Follow it for 3.3 mi. (5.3 km) and make another right turn onto Roseman Road. Follow this road 0.8 mi. (1.3 km) and turn right again onto Forestdale Road. Continue 2.1 mi. (3.4 km) down Forestdale Road. The road levels out here after a short downhill. Look for bold red blazes on trees on the left, marking the trail opening onto the road.

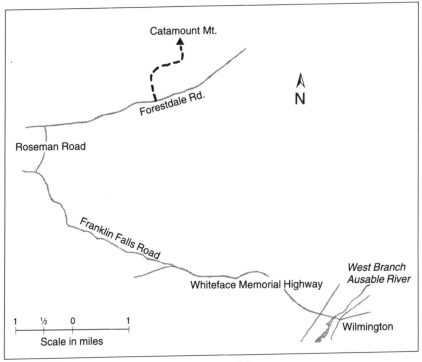

Catamount (9)

The trail is easily followed, although not marked. After approximately 0.2 mi. (0.3 km) the trail turns left at a metal pipe property marker. Shortly thereafter it emerges into a former field, now covered with striking mosses and blueberry bushes. The rocky wall of Catamount appears ahead. The trail bears right shortly before the end of the open area and enters a beech, birch, and maple woods. One unusual tree, soon seen on the right, we called "five-star birch" for the five large trunks radiating from a single bole at ground level.

The trail begins to ascend gently, then descends to cross a brook at about 0.8 mi. (1.3 km). Now the trail starts to climb in earnest. From here on there are some very steep sections. In many spots short legs may need help up very big steps, but the rewards of persevering are substantial. Unlike so many Adirondack trails, this one affords almost constant views on its upper half. The top of Catamount has been burned twice, and large areas of bare rock are the result. Rock cairns mark the way, and one comes to appreciate their guidance. While there are probably many possible routes that would lead to the summit, the frequent steep rock faces limit easy passage. The cairns mark the best route. Especially on the return, it is essential to keep to the marked route.

Scrambling up bare rock is lots of fun. The rock is quite rough, which helps to prevent slipping, at least in dry weather. The highlight of the scramble is the "chimney," a 30-ft. (9-m) very steep crevice where less resistant rock has been eroded away between two walls of granitic gneiss. Not long after passing through this feature the top of the "cobble" is reached. Whiteface Mountain dominates the views to the south. The views are excellent in all directions except to the north, where the bulk of the true summit of Catamount lies about 0.5 mi. (0.8 km) farther on. A very satisfying hike could be ended here, especially if the blueberries which are abundant on the "cobble" are ripe. The half-mile to the summit is mostly across rock, with some areas of scrub woods. Following the cairns is very important here, especially as you descend. The views from the summit are even more impressive. Taylor Pond, Silver Lake Mountain, and Lyon Mountain can be seen to the north.

Counting the toads in all colors and sizes and searching for fungi in varied shades helped time pass on this lengthy hike. The rock cairns fascinated our children and they enjoyed scouting out the next one to guide our way. Meeting the brook on the way out presented an irresistible chance to cool hot and tired feet in frigid, clear water. We are told that on busy weekends this mountain may have fifty or more climbers in a day, but it remains one of the less frequented gems in the northern Adirondacks.

Tupper Lake, Cranberry Lake & Northwest Section

Roads are scarcer in this remote corner of the Adirondack Park. The peaks are smaller and lakes of relatively greater significance. Opportunities for true wilderness experiences abound in large areas of forest which have recovered from extensive logging in the early part of this century. Timber is still important to the region, but now canoeing, camping, and hiking are important as well.

OTHER ATTRACTIONS IN THIS SECTION:

- St. Regis Canoe Area
- Natural Bridge Caverns, Natural Bridge; guided tours (315-644-4810)
- Woodsmen's Field Days, Tupper Lake; held second full weekend of July
- Adirondack Fish Cultural Station, Saranac Inn (518-891-3358)
- Public Campgrounds (call 1-800-456-2267 for reservations)
    Cranberry Lake—east of the village
    Fish Creek and Rollins Pond—near Lake Clear
    Forked Lake—south of Long Lake
    Lake Eaton—north of Long Lake

10. Lampson Falls and Grass River Trail
Round-trip to falls: 0.8 mi. (1.3 km)
Round-trip including Grass River Trail: 2.8 mi. (4.5 km)
Elevation change: Minimal
Map: West Pierrepont 7.5'

The base of these roaring falls on the Grass River is a great destination for a picnic lunch, with the possibility of further explorations along the shores of this beautiful river.

Trailhead: Access is on the Clare Road. From NY 3 at Fine, take the Degrasse-Fine Road into Degrasse. Turn right and continue 4.5 mi. (7.2 km) north of Degrasse to the trailhead on the left. If coming from the north end of the Clare Road, it is 5.8 mi. (9.3 km) south of the intersection of Clare Road and the Pierrepont-Russell Road. A sign for the Grass River State Forest on the west side of the road marks the entrance. Park along the road.

The trail begins at a barrier and continues down a fairly level dirt road. On a late July walk there were brilliant splashes of red from the fruiting bunchberries. You will begin to hear the falls before you see them. The first main herd path off to the left leads to the top of the falls. Shortly afterwards, another trail off to the left works its way to the base of the falls. The bare rocks ringing the pool make a great spot for a picnic lunch. Many signs of places where people have camped nearby are visible. Be careful with young children near the water's edge. When the water was low in midsummer, we were able to find some safe sandy spots near the base of the falls where we could get our feet wet and cool down.

Continuing the walk downstream is well worth the effort. Work your way downstream until you pick up a trail with red trail markers. The trail stays close to the water. There are several wet areas

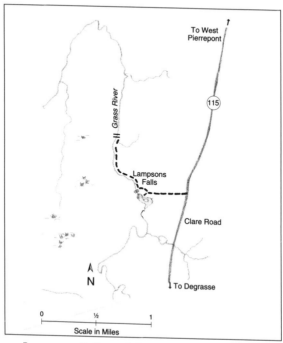

Lampson Falls and Grass River Trail (10)

where log bridges help keep feet dry. Ferns, mushrooms, and wildflowers are to be found everywhere. There is an area of tall grasses about 0.4 mi. (0.6 km) down the trail. Be careful of the beaver plunge holes on the river side of the trail. At about 0.8 mi. (1.3 km) a sizable wooden bridge crosses the river. This would also be a nice choice for a picnic spot. The Grass River contracts from a 75-ft. (23-m) width to a 20-ft. (6-m) classic flume under the bridge.

The walk can be extended by continuing downstream after you cross the bridge (the west side) for about 1.2 mi. (1.9 km) until you reach private land. The trail passes many small waterfalls and cascades. Return along the same trail.

> *Lots of time can be spent playing with frogs in the small pools of water that collect in the rocks by the water's edge. We'll never forget the joy in our five-year-old friend's eyes as he held his first frog on this trip. Kids just love watching for these interesting creatures. The frogs can be found in all sizes and shades of brown and green. The frogs don't seem to mind being picked up gently to be observed, but as we have told our boys many times, "No, they cannot be put in your pocket and taken home for a pet!" The older boys were good about explaining to younger children that frogs should not be held too tightly, that they need to stay wet, and that they should be held close to the ground so they won't get hurt if they wiggle free.*

11. Fernow Forest Self-Guided Nature Trail

Round-trip loop: 1.1 mi. (1.8 km)
Elevation change: Minimal
Map: St. Regis 15' or Upper Saranac Lake metric

This trail provides the contrast of a forest of mixed native hardwoods and an overgrown conifer plantation. It offers an occasion to think about human projects that change existing conditions. Fernow's experiment aimed at completely altering the forest tract from mixed hardwood to pine-spruce. Hikers can see the clear line separating the two types of woods. The brochure at the trail register describes this as a successful experiment. What do you think? Whatever you decide, the trail provides a pleasant and easy stroll.

Trailhead: The trail begins on NY 30, just 0.8 mi. (1.3 km) north of the intersection of NY 3 and NY 30. It is a short distance from Wawbeek Corners. The parking area is on the west side of the road, marked by a large sign.

A short way along the trail there is a sign indicating that the trail is maintained by the Paul Smiths Student Chapter of the Society of American Foresters. Just beyond is a trail register with brochures describing the history of the trail as well as descriptions of numbered and lettered stations. Benches along the trail provide opportunities to stop and observe.

> *There were a few wildflowers along the forest floor when we hiked this trail in late July. Earlier in the spring, blooms would be more plentiful. It's a nice opportunity to point out various tree types and discuss the cycles of life within a forest, as you view trees in all the different stages of growth and decay. There are also huge moss-covered boulders scattered about, indicating glacial activity. Children are tempted to race up these boulders, destroying the fragile mosses. This is an opportunity for parents to discuss our impact on nature.*

12. Bear Mountain Bog

Round-trip: 3.4 mi. (5.4 km)
Elevation change: Minimal
Map: Cranberry Lake 7.5′ or Cranberry Lake 15′

This is an easy forest walk leading to two 250-ft. (75-m) boardwalks over wetlands. It is a fine hike for beginners, who will find plenty to see along the way. Numbers are posted on trees for an interpretive walk, but copies of the brochure are not always available. We tried to recreate the guide by guessing what the significant feature might be at each number.

Trailhead: Entrance to Cranberry Lake Public Campground is on NY 3 at the east end of the village of Cranberry Lake. Park near campsite 29 (get a map at the gate). A register with an excellent map of the trails in the Cranberry Lake area is at the trailhead.

The trail to Bear Mountain Bog branches left from the Bear Mountain trail at about 0.2 mi. (0.3 km). The first mile is through hardwoods, with very little understory, giving an exceptionally open feeling. At about 0.9 mi. (1.4 km) the trail joins an old tote road, which it follows briefly. The trail soon turns right off the road and begins dropping. It reaches the first boardwalk at about 1.4 mi. (2.2 km). It's not often that you get to walk dry-footed straight through a wetland. A 0.3-mi. (0.5-km) section of trail brings you to a second boardwalk over even wetter terrain. The carpeted floor of sphagnum moss and the denseness of the vegetation are in sharp contrast to the woods through which you've just walked.

The trail continues to a junction with a trail south from NY 3, but turning around after the second boardwalk is suggested.

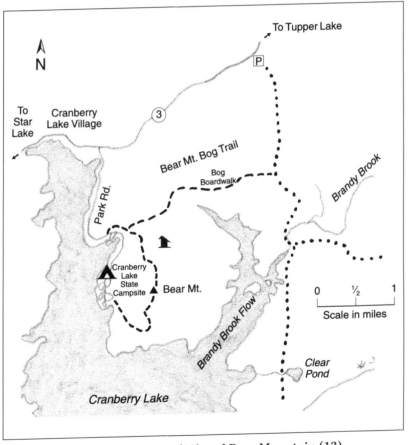

Bear Mountain Bog (12) and Bear Mountain (13)

13. Bear Mountain

Round-trip: 3.4 mi. (5.4 km)
Elevation change: 660 ft. (201 m)
Map: Cranberry Lake 7.5' or Cranberry Lake 15'

A nice climb for younger hikers. (See map, page 69) The shortest access is within the Cranberry Lake Public Campground.

Trailhead: Entrance to the campground is on NY 3 at the east end of the village of Cranberry Lake. Park near Campsite 29 (get a map at the gate). A register with an excellent map of the trails in the Cranberry Lake area is at the trailhead.

The trail up Bear Mountain is well used and fairly easy for most of its length. The beginning is quite gentle, though full of roots and rocks to hop on and over. The trail to Bear Mountain Bog turns left at 0.2 mi. (0.3 km). There is a lean-to on the left at 0.8 mi. (1.3 km) and somewhat steeper climbing begins. A short pitch over bare rock is passed at about 1.1 mi. (1.8 km). At 1.2 mi. (1.9 km) the trail reaches the crest of the mountain. Two large boulders offer scrambling and photo opportunities, but no views. Behind and beneath the boulder on the right (west) side is a bivouac site. As with much Adirondack rock, these boulders are rough, with interesting banding. The trail proceeds 0.4 mi. (0.6 km) along the crest to a point where an outcrop offers wonderful views over Cranberry Lake and the hills to the west.

The choice is now between retracing the trail or continuing down the steep trail ahead, which leads to the southern end of the campground. A long walk on the road through the park will bring you back to the trailhead. We chose to retrace our steps.

A six-year-old friend hiking with us on this trail insisted on carrying his own backpack, which was large but empty, except for a magnifying lens and a water bottle. He stopped on several occasions to view a rock or some tree bark more carefully with the lens. He soon realized the pack was slowing him down and handed it to his mom. She quietly shouldered it and let him run on rather than lecture about responsibility. This hike could be recalled at a later time to suggest a different way of carrying the hand lens so that no pack would be needed. It was interesting to see the young hiker appreciate that one aspect of hiking is careful observation of surroundings. A small, inexpensive hand lens would be a nice addition to your list of basics.

14. Mt. Arab
Round-trip: 2.0 mi. (3.2 km)
Elevation change: 760 ft. (232 m)
Map: Piercefield 7.5', Tupper Lake 15', or Piercefield metric

Note that this trail is closed during big-game rifle season in the fall.

Trains were important in the Adirondacks during the era of large-scale logging and high-society vacationing. Some of the rail lines are still present and sporadic attempts have been made to run "sight-seeing" trains on some of them. From the summit of Mt. Arab the Remsen–Lake Placid tracks can be seen snaking through the trees to the east of Mt. Arab Lake. At present, one can only imagine this trip, with a little help from the splendid view looking south from the summit of Mt. Arab.

Trailhead: From NY 3 turn south on Conifer Road. This is 7.0 mi (11.2 km) west of the intersection of NY 3 and NY 30 in Tupper Lake or 10.4 mi. (16.7 km) east of Seveys Corners. Follow Conifer Road 1.8 mi. (2.9 km) to Eagle Crag Lake Road on the left. Take this road 0.9 mi. (1.4 km) to the trailhead on the left, about 0.3 mi. (0.5 km) after crossing the railroad tracks. Park in the parking area across the road from the trailhead.

The trail climbs quickly, entering Forest Preserve land at 0.3 mi. (0.5 km). It continues fairly steeply until shortly below the summit, where it passes by large granite outcrops. The trail circles around to reach the summit clearing at 1.0 mi. (1.6 km). The rail line runs to the south, at the base of the mountain, with Mt. Arab Lake and Eagle Crag Lake to its west. The region southwest of Mt. Arab is one of the wildest in the Park. The Bog River, Lows Lake, and Lake Lila adjoin the large Five Ponds Wilderness Area. Perhaps best known as canoe country, this area also offers extended wilderness camping possibilities. From the tower there are views of the High Peaks region and Tupper Lake village to the east. Its restoration (1999) is an example of cooperative efforts that have saved several towers in the Adirondacks in recent years.

15. Floodwood Mountain

Round-trip: 3.4 mi. (5.4 km)
Elevation change: 620 ft. (189 m)
Map: St. Regis 15' or Upper Saranac Lake metric

Floodwood Mountain used to belong to the Bergen County, New Jersey Boy Scouts and was added to the Forest Preserve in 1990. A Boy Scout right-of-way grants access to the public trail. The hike is not very difficult and offers some nice views.

Trailhead: Access is off the Floodwood Road on the west side of NY 30 halfway between Paul Smiths and Tupper Lake. Turn at the Saranac Inn Golf Course. Take Floodwood Road, a wide dirt road, for 6.4 mi. (10.2 km) to a sign for the Floodwood Scout Reservation. Turn left at the sign. Within 0.3 mi. (0.5 km) there is a well-marked public parking area.

Turning left from the parking area, you come to a road barrier. Go around this to the beginning of the public trail. Follow the road for about 0.7 mi. (1.1 km) to a sign on the right indicating 1.0 mi. (1.6 km) to Floodwood Mountain. There are two sizable cherry trees on the right shortly after you begin this part of the trail and a couple of streams to cross by rock hopping. The trail, marked with red disks, climbs easily through hardwood forests for the first 0.5 mi. (0.8 km). The second half-mile is steeper as you ascend the north slope of the mountain.

An open rock area awaits you at the top with views to the north of Azure and St. Regis Mountains. Better views and a better picnic spot are found by continuing along the trail several hundred yards to the southern summit. In season, blueberries are plentiful.

On this outing, our boys and one of their friends hiked on ahead at a brisk pace, talking and playing the whole way. A second friend lagged behind with, "My feet hurt," and "I can't do it." She seemed to have one reason after another for a tear or complaint. Her mom and I provided water, encouragement, and some GORP, and she rather reluctantly reached the summit. We all ate lunch there and she was a changed person, the happy hiker she usually is. Her energy stores were just too low. Having started the hike so close to noon, we realized in hindsight it would have been better to offer lunch before starting out. It was amazing how energetic she was on the way down. We cannot always use adult body signals to know what kids need, and kids cannot always verbalize what they need.

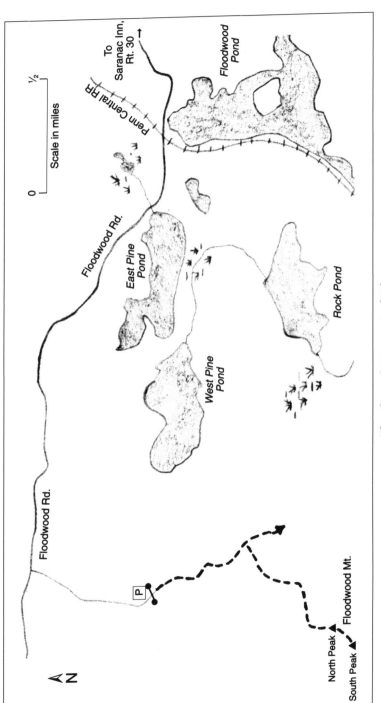

Floodwood Mountain (15)

16. Panther Mountain

Round-trip: 1.2 mi. (1.9 km)
Elevation change: 500 ft. (152 m)
Map: Long Lake 15' or Tupper Lake metric

This is a terrific first hike for children. The climbing starts right away, but is never too steep, and the views are very satisfying.

Trailhead: Access is on NY 3 between Tupper Lake and Saranac Lake, roughly 1.5 mi. (2.4 km) east of the intersection of NY 3 and NY 30. The parking area is on the south side of the road and the trail begins across the road. Use special care crossing the highway.

The trailhead marker indicates the trail is 0.9 mi. (1.4 km) long, but the distance is actually 0.6 mi. (1.0 km). The trail is very easy to follow and climbs at a steady rate through nice forests. There are conifers at the lower levels, changing to mixed hardwoods. The trail arrives at a bald summit. There are blueberries and wildflowers at the top as well as nice views. One can see Ampersand Mountain, Panther Pond, and Tupper Lake. From the parking area, a short trail leads to the shore of Panther Pond.

17. Stone Valley Trails

Round-trip loop: 7.5 mi. (12.0 km)
Elevation change: Minimal
Possible smaller trips of almost any distance
Map: Colton 7.5'

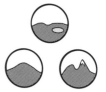

The Stone Valley Cooperative Recreational Area is just outside the Adirondack Park. Trails are maintained by Niagara Mohawk Power Corporation, the Laurentian Chapter of the Adirondack Mountain Club, and the St. Lawrence County Youth Conservation Corps. Trails follow both sides of the Raquette River as it flows from Colton to Hannawa Falls, sometimes on a high bank with fine views of the rushing water, and sometimes right along the shore. As is true of any walk close to the water, there are places where a close eye should be kept on young hikers. The trail is well marked with blue diamond-shaped markers and there are many possible starting points. The beginning of each section of trail is described below, so you can plan the hike that most appeals to you. The trail is roughly 3.2 mi. (5.1 km)

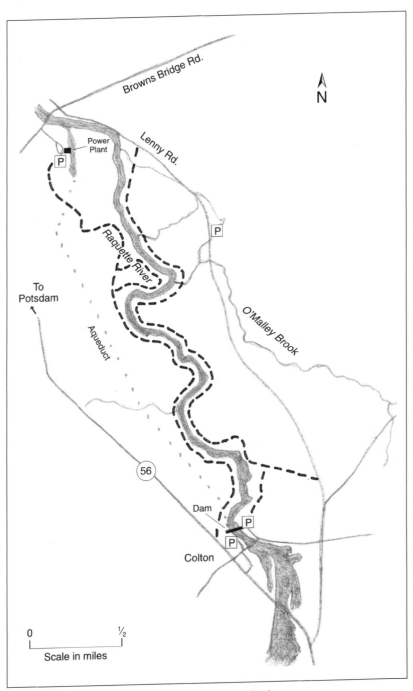

Stone Valley Trails (17)

long on each side of the river and may be completed as a loop. The most popular part is probably the first 2.0 mi. (3.2 km) on the east side of the Colton trailhead.

A few words of caution: the water levels of the river are controlled by Niagara Mohawk, and they can change quickly, with little warning. This should not be of great concern if you stay on the trail, but be alert if you decide to picnic on rocks by the river's edge. Swimming or playing in the water is inadvisable for the same reason.

Colton Trailhead (East Side): From NY 56 in the town of Colton, turn east towards the river at the Town Library. Cross the bridge and immediately turn left. Continue straight ahead until you reach a dirt parking area. Two enormous millstones mark the entrance to the trail.

The trail is narrow in places as it traverses the steep valley walls. In a short while there is an intersection with a wider path. Turn left and you soon come to the river. There is a large area of open rock extending into the river, which is very popular with picnickers. Depending on the season and level of water, this is a place where people like to get their feet wet. Attention is needed with young children.

The trail continues downstream, to the north, along a nice bed of pine needles. There is a section of steps up a steep slope to a height with nice views down to the river. Several trails to the right lead to a dirt road paralleling the river on the east. The trail stays along the river and is indicated by blue diamond-shaped markers.

Along this section of trail there are several signs with information about geological features. At about 1.8 mi. (2.9 km) the trail reaches a bridge crossing O'Malley Brook and a large open clearing. Cross the bridge and continue along the river. The trail ends on a dirt road, about a quarter of a mile from the Browns Bridge Road. If you are doing the whole circuit, continue left down the road, cross the bridge and pick up the trail at the power station on the other side. (There is a sign leading to the trail.)

Hannawa Falls Trailhead (East Side): From NY 56 turn east onto the Browns Bridge Road, about 2.0 mi. (3.2 km) north of Colton and 7.0 mi. (11.2 km) south of Potsdam. Just after the bridge turn right onto Lenny Road. In about 0.3 mi. (0.5 km) there is a sign on the right indicating the start of the trail. This is the end of the east bank trail described above. Park along the side of the road.

Hannawa Falls Trailhead (West Side): From NY 56 turn east onto the Browns Bridge Road about 2.0 mi. (3.2 km) north of Colton and 7.0 mi. (11.2 km) south of Potsdam. Just before the bridge there is a trail sign indicating a right turn off the road. A dirt road leads to one of Niagara Mohawk's power stations, with a marked parking area.

The trail starts on a dirt road to the right. In a few minutes the trail turns left. (The dirt road would lead you to Colton in about 3.0 mi. or 4.8 km). The trail is wide here and covered with pine needles. The wide path soon veers to the right but the trail continues straight ahead, marked by blue diamond markers. The trail leads over a few wet sections, with logs across a stream. The river appears to the left and the trail narrows as it follows the river. Use caution in sections that are very close to the shore, especially if the water is high.

After following the river for a couple of miles, you will notice the stone foundation from an old tannery on the left. About 2.7 mi. (4.3 km) from the trailhead there is a wooden bridge across the penstock. Turn left on the dirt road. Cross the bridge in town to continue the trail on the other side of the river. (See Colton Trailhead East Side above.)

Colton Trailhead (West Side): From NY 56 in the town of Colton, turn east towards the river at the Town Library. Turn left just before the bridge. There is a marked parking area. Walk along the dirt road past a barrier to a wooden bridge on the right, crossing the penstock. This is the end point of the west bank trail described above.

Lake Placid, Saranac Lake, & Paul Smiths Section

As the site of two Winter Olympics (1932 and 1980), Lake Placid is perhaps the most renowned location in the Adirondacks. Vacationing and winter sports are traditional to this region. Hiking and camping equipment suppliers are well represented in the larger communities. Saranac Lake was the site of early research and therapy for tuberculosis, and is still a center for health care in the region. The town of Paul Smiths is named for the proprietor of one of the hotels catering to the first wave of Adirondack tourists. The large lakes and early popularity of this region have made it a central point of interest for visitors to the Park.

OTHER ATTRACTIONS IN THIS SECTION:

- Six Nations Indian Museum, Onchiota (518-891-0769)
- White Pine Camp on Osgood Pond; summer White House of Calvin Coolidge (518-327-3030)
- Olympic Ski Jump Complex and Olympic Ice Arena, Lake Placid (Olympic Regional Development Authority, 518-523-1655)
- Whiteface Mountain Ski Center (chair lift rides) and Whiteface Memorial Highway, Wilmington (518-946-2223)
- High Falls Gorge, NY 86, Wilmington (518-946-2278)
- John Brown Farm State Historic Site, Lake Placid (518-523-3900)
- Lake Placid Center for the Arts, Lake Placid (518-523-2512)
- Santa's Workshop, Wilmington (518-946-2212)
- Adirondak Loj Campground, Adirondak Loj Road, Lake Placid (518-523-3441)
- Public Beach—Saranac Lake
- Public Campgrounds (call 1-800-456-2267 for reservations)
  Meadowbrook—Ray Brook
  Wilmington Notch—NY 86 north of Lake Placid

18. Brewster Peninsula Nature Trails

About 2.0 mi. (3.2 km) of interconnecting trails
Elevation change: Minimal
Map: Lake Placid 15' or Lake Placid metric

The loops that make up this trail system are well known to cross-country skiers in the area, but they also make very pleasant walking at other times of the year. The 133 acres owned by the state on the peninsula jutting into Lake Placid have three interconnected trails known as the Lakeshore Trail (blue markers), Ridge Trail (yellow

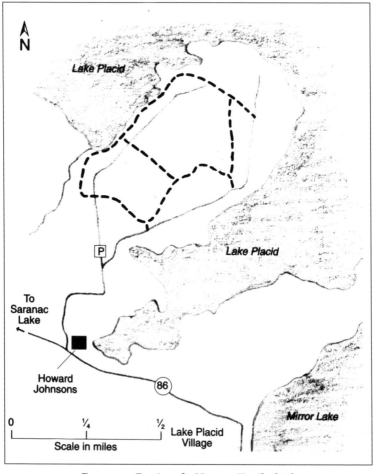

Brewster Peninsula Nature Trails (18)

markers), and Boundary Trail (red markers). The Jack Rabbit trail, a long cross-country ski trail, also connects with this trail network. A guide to the Peninsula Trail System can be picked up at the Lake Placid Visitor's Bureau, near the Olympic Center in downtown Lake Placid.

Trailhead: A small sign on NY 86 between the Howard Johnson Restaurant and Howard Johnson Motor Inn directs you up a narrow road, paved at first. After about a 0.5-mi. (0.8-km) drive down this winding road, a barricaded dirt road forks to the left. Park here and walk past the barricade down this road 0.1 mi. (0.2 km) to the junction with the Boundary Trail.

Turning left leads quickly to the shore of Lake Placid near the spillway. Turning right at a junction near the spillway, the trail continues to the right with the shore close on its left. There are good views of Whiteface Mountain through the cedars that border the lake. About 0.3 mi. (0.5 km) of very pleasant walking along the shore leads to another intersection. Turn right to regain the road. Other loops are possible on the east side of the peninsula. More than 2.0 mi. (3.2 km) of trails, mostly flat and pleasant afford walks of varied lengths. Watch for mountain bikers, who also frequent these trails.

19. Visitor Interpretive Center at Paul Smiths

   Round-trip distance possibilities range from
      0.6 mi. (1.0 km) to 1.2 mi. (1.9 km),
         with the option of combining several trails
   Elevation change: Minimal
   Map: St. Regis 7.5', St. Regis 15', or St. Regis Mountain metric

The Interpretive Center provides a wonderful introduction to the Adirondacks and a great place to begin hiking if you have never hiked before. The well-maintained trails have signs providing information along the way, so you can make the hikes as educational as you like. Some trails (especially the Barnum Brook Trail) may even be managed with strollers.

   Guided walks are offered at various times during the day, as are lectures, audiovisual presentations, and demonstrations. Tables are provided for picnicking and there is a very comfortable building with restrooms, displays, and a gift shop. Be sure to visit the butterfly house during the summer months. The things you learn will help you be more knowledgeable about nature as you hike in other areas of the Park. At the Center, we learned about "nature's plow" (when a large tree is uprooted and, in falling, pulls up all that lay attached to its roots), something we now notice over and over on our hikes.

The Interpretive Center is located off NY 30 about 0.9 mi. (1.4 km) north of Paul Smiths College. It is open year-round. A detailed map of the trail system is available at the Center. Below is a brief description of the trails, giving the length of each as well as the round-trip distance from the main building. Note that the Heron Marsh and Barnum Brook Trails, probably the easiest for very young children, are loops from the main building. The other trails piggyback on these two. More information can be obtained at the Center itself, or by calling 518-327-3000.

- **Heron Marsh Trail**: 0.8-mi. (1.3-km) loop. There are two boardwalks and an elevated viewing tower on this trail, with vistas of a freshwater marsh and Jenkins Mountain in the background.
- **Shingle Mill Falls Trail**: 0.6 mi. (1.0 km); 1.4-mi. (2.2-km) loop from the main building, using the Heron Marsh Trail as connector. The trail includes a 300-ft. (91-m) pontoon bridge over a marsh and passes a waterfall along the way.
- **Forest Ecology Trail**: 1.2 mi. (1.9 km); 2.4-mi. (3.8-km) loop from the main building, using parts of the Barnum Brook and Shingle Mill Falls Trails. This trail goes through a variety of forest habitats and crosses a peat bog over a 900-ft. (274-m) boardwalk.
- **Silviculture Trail**: 1.0-mi. (1.6-km) loop from Keese Mill Road access; 3.5-mi. (5.6-km) loop from the main building. The trail is reached from a separate parking area off Keese Mill Road (the shortest route) or from the Forest Ecology Trail. The loop passes through natural and planted forests and tells of various forestry systems and harvesting methods.
- **Barnum Brook Trail**: 0.6-mi. (1.0-km) loop. This is a wheelchair-accessible route. It passes an active beaver colony and crosses over Barnum Brook. It is the only trail open for hiking in the winter, when the other trails are open for cross-country skiing.

20. Red Dot Trail

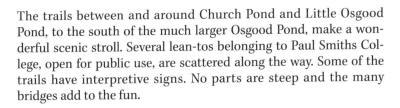

Round-trip: 2.6 mi. (4.2 km)
Elevation change: Minimal
Map: Gabriels 7.5′ and St. Regis 7.5′, Saranac Lake 15′,
   or Bloomingdale metric

The trails between and around Church Pond and Little Osgood Pond, to the south of the much larger Osgood Pond, make a wonderful scenic stroll. Several lean-tos belonging to Paul Smiths College, open for public use, are scattered along the way. Some of the trails have interpretive signs. No parts are steep and the many bridges add to the fun.

Trailhead: Park in the lot behind St. Gabriels Church at the intersection of NY 30 and NY 192 in Paul Smiths.

Two trails lead into this trail system from the parking lot: the Jack Rabbit Spur Trail, and, several yards to the east (right), the Spur to Red Dot Trails and Cathedral Pines. The latter trail (yellow markers) leads to the west edge of Church Pond in about 150 yds. At 0.3 mi. (0.5 km) it crosses a major trail and shortly thereafter joins the red-marked Jackrabbit Trail. This is a long-distance cross-country ski trail that extends east to the village of Keene and is marked with distinctive, red trail signs. Also at this juncture, a spur trail to Cathedral Pines branches right. This short trail leads to several benches in a stand of large pine trees. Look up!

Continuing on the Jackrabbit Trail you reach the Church Pond lean-to at about 0.8 mi. (1.3 km) and shortly after that a bridge over a canal. Several explanations have been offered for why this canal and others in the area were constructed. The most frequently heard one is that they were intended to provide canoe access to the churches from Osgood Pond.

Just past the bridge the trail forks; bear left to follow a trail with red paint blazes. In the next 0.5 mi. (0.8 km) this trail passes a pond and then follows another canal on the left, before ending at a beach and parking area and a bay of Osgood Pond. Retrace your steps for a total walk of about 2.6 mi. (4.2 km).

Because the walk to the lean-to is short and an easy one for children, it is a good choice for a first overnight experience. Some children may be fearful of doing things in the dark such as meal

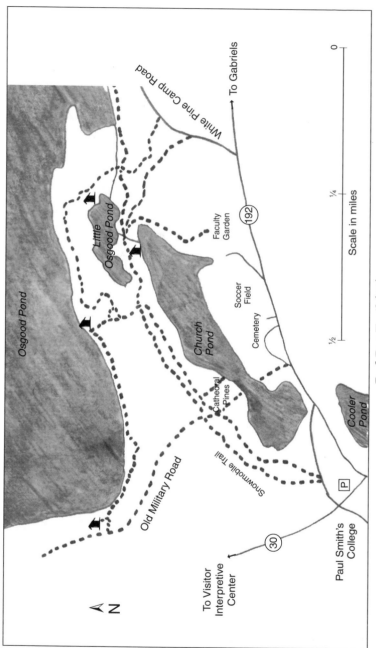

Red Dot Trail (20)

preparation, eating, or relieving themselves. Lots of assuring talk may be needed to alleviate their fears.

21. Black Pond

Round-trip: 3.0 mi. (4.8 km)
Elevation change: Minimal
Map: St. Regis 7.5′ and Gabriels 7.5′, St. Regis 15′,
   or St. Regis Mountain metric

The western shore of this attractive pond at the base of Jenkins Mountain is bordered by a long esker. Much of the walk is between pond and esker. The land is managed by the Visitor Interpretive Center at Paul Smiths. There are several lean-tos along the pond, nice as picnic or rest spots, but not available for overnight use.

Trailhead: From NY 30 in Paul Smiths, turn west onto Keese Mills Road. Drive 2.5 mi. (4.0 km) to Keese Mills. The St. Regis Presbyterian Church is on the south side of the road. There is a parking area on the opposite side of the road, just across the stream. The sign indicates "Parking Area for Anglers" and designates it as a day-use area with no camping or campfires allowed.

In just 100 ft. (30 m) there is a small canoe dock on the right and a trail register on the left. The path, which is not formally marked, follows along the west bank of the outlet until reaching Black Pond in about 0.2 mi. (0.3 km). The trail climbs slightly and circles towards the north. There is a small wooden bridge to a lean-to. Another lean-to can be seen across the pond. The path continues beneath the esker and stays very close to the shore. Be careful with very young hikers. There are some wooden planks over wetter areas and care with footing is sometimes needed. There is a landing dock at 0.8 mi. (1.3 km) near the northern end of the pond, for canoeists wishing to portage from Black Pond to Long Pond.

The trail widens here as it follows the stream connecting the two ponds. About 200 yd. (183 m) along, a path goes right, crossing a fish barrier on the stream. Turn right to continue hiking south along the east shore of Black Pond. This path leads to a bridge across a channel separating the main body of Black Pond from an eastern lobe. There is a lean-to with no floor here, but if you continue a bit over some wet footing, you arrive at the lean-to sighted from across the

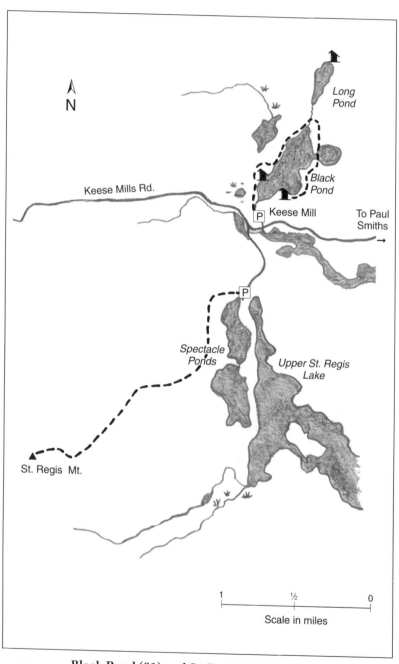

Black Pond (21) and St. Regis Mountain (27)

pond at the start of the trip. This makes a pleasant rest area before the return trip. There are great views of Jenkins Mountain to the north, and St. Regis Mountain to the southwest.

At the fish barrier between the two ponds, it is possible to continue north along Long Pond. There is a lean-to at its northern end.

A walk around a pond that does not involve much climbing can be a nice change for small hikers. There are a few places where one can climb to the top of the esker and look down at the pond on one side and a gully on the other. An esker is a long narrow ridge of coarse gravel deposited by a stream which flowed in an ice-walled valley of a glacier once covering an area. In season, you will see raspberries, blueberries, and touch-me-nots with seedpods ready to burst open at your touch.

22. Owen and Copperas Ponds

Round-trip: 3.2 mi. (5.1 km)
Elevation change: 295 ft. (90 m)
Map: Lake Placid 7.5', Lake Placid 15', or Lake Placid metric

This is a pleasant walk involving a few short, steep sections. The trail offers a mix of woods and attractive ponds. Be on the lookout for sundews from June to August. There is a lean-to at Copperas Pond that makes a good picnic destination or a possible first backpacking trip for children. We describe the southerly approach here, which is the more popular route. The approach 1.0 mi. (1.6 km) further north on NY 86 leads to Copperas Pond in about 0.5 mi. (0.8 km).

Trailhead: Take NY 86 for 5.0 mi. (8.0 km) from its junction with NY 73 in Lake Placid Village, or 3.9 mi. (6.2 km) south from the entrance to Whiteface Mountain Ski Center. The trail begins on the east side of the road and is marked with a small DEC sign.

The blue marked trail leads gradually up, staying near the right bank of Owen Pond Brook, and reaches the northwest corner of Owen Pond at 0.6 mi. (1.0 km). The trail follows the shore of the

pond to the northeast corner at 0.7 mi. (1.1 km). Here it veers away
to the left and climbs steeply. At about 1.0 mi. (1.6 km) the trail
swings right. It descends steeply to the shore of Copperas Pond at
1.3 mi. (2.1 km). There is an excellent view of Whiteface Mountain
from the pleasant open spaces on the shore here. The trail continues
along the shore. At 1.4 mi. (2.2 km) there is a junction with a yellow
marked trail to Winch Pond. The trail straight ahead leads along the
shore, with a 0.1 mi. (0.2 km) spur going left, to the Copperas Pond
lean-to at 1.6 mi. (2.6 km).

If a loop is desired, the trail to the right at the junction passed on
the way to the lean-to reaches the highway in another 0.5 mi. (0.8
km). You will either need a second car at the northern trailhead, or
plan to walk about a mile along the highway to return to the start.

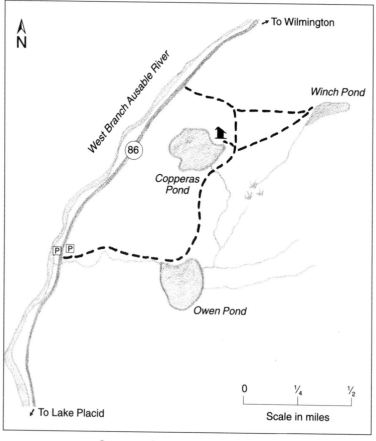

Owen and Copperas Ponds (22)

On this hike we had one child in a backpack while the other was a young walker. We were accompanied by an older woman who is a member of our local ADK chapter. It made us realize that many of the hikes suitable for very young hikers are also well suited to older folks, maybe grandparents, who are new to hiking or who can no longer hike as vigorously as when they were younger.

23. Baker Mountain

Round-trip: 1.8 mi. (2.9 km)
Elevation Change: 900 ft. (274 m)
Map: McKenzie Mountain 7.5', Saranac Lake 15',
or Saranac Lake metric

This short hike has long been a favorite among Saranac Lakers. It's an easy climb, has fine views, and the trailhead is within walking distance of many village homes.

Trailhead: Entering Saranac Lake on NY 86 from Lake Placid, turn right at the T-intersection onto McKenzie Pond Road. Drive over the railroad tracks and turn left on Pine Street. Cross the tracks again and proceed to East Pine Street. Turn right onto East Pine Street, cross the wooden overpass and continue to the north end of Moody Pond. A small DEC sign marks the trailhead. Park along the road.

The trail is quite well used and not hard to follow. It starts on an old tote road but soon diverges to the right. Some 75 yd. (69 m) later it bears left, climbs past an old quarry, then turns right. At 0.2 mi. (0.3 km) a house is visible on the right. The climbing is stiff, but a brief respite at 0.4 mi. (0.6 km) prepares you for another steep section. The trail splits at 0.6 mi. (1.0 km), with the paths rejoining 0.2 mi. (0.3 km) below the summit.

From the partly wooded top there are good views to the east and south, including McKenzie Pond almost at the base of the mountain due east, Haystack Mountain just beyond, and many high peaks to the south in the distance. A short path goes north from the summit to a cliff from which Debar and St. Regis Mountains can be seen to the north.

24. Mt. Jo

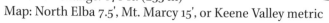

Round-trip: 2.2 mi. (3.5 km)
Elevation change: 670 ft. (233 m)
Map: North Elba 7.5', Mt. Marcy 15', or Keene Valley metric

Mt. Jo is often the first peak climbed by children of avid Adirondack hikers. Located on the shore of Heart Lake, the most popular starting point for hikes into the High Peaks, Mt. Jo is an obvious choice for a beginning hike. The trail is short, but steep, leaving no doubt that a mountain has been climbed. The view of Heart Lake and the highest peaks in the Park just beyond should inspire any hiker to further goals. But be warned: Popularity of this trail access means parking is often highly competitive.

Trailhead: Turn south from NY 73, 4.0 mi. (6.4 km) southeast of Lake Placid Village. There is a sign for the Adirondak Loj as well as a large DEC sign reading "Trails to the High Peaks." At 4.8 mi. (7.7 km) there is a small entrance booth. There is a daily parking fee.

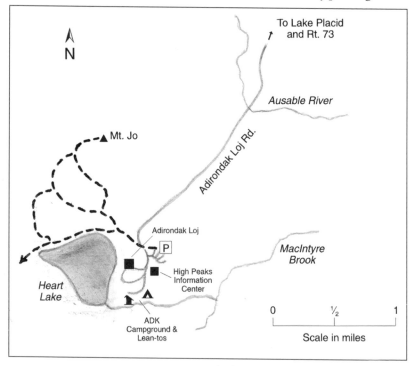

Mt. Jo (24)

The parking lot is left past the booth. The trail starts west of the turnaround at the entrance station.

A short way down this trail, signs mark the turn for Mt. Jo, to the right. After 0.3 mi. (0.5 km) of moderate climbing, a junction is reached. The longer trail goes left, and the shorter, steeper trail to the right. Let your children have their choice—either one is fine (0.2 mi. [0.3 km] difference). The trails join for the final 0.1 mi. (0.2 km) to the summit. On the longer route, avoid the blue blazed trail which branches left at 0.7 mi. (1.1 km).

The list of peaks in view from the top includes all the best known summits in the Adirondacks. The sparkling water of Heart Lake and the deep notch of Indian Pass are also impressive. The climb can be done as a partial loop by taking one branch of the trail on the way up, and the other on the way down.

25. Rocky Falls

Round-trip: 4.8 mi. (7.7 km)
Elevation change: Minimal
Map: Mt. Marcy 15' or Keene Valley metric

Heart Lake is a popular starting point for hikes into the High Peaks Wilderness Area, including the shortest routes to Mt. Marcy, Algonquin, Colden, and others of the highest peaks. Several fine and less heavily used trails are well suited for the younger hiker. The hike to Rocky Falls is a very pleasant ramble that can be extended to Scott Clearing if a longer hike is wanted. The impressive cliffs of Indian Pass (2.2 mi. [3.5 km] beyond Scott Clearing) are a 6.0 mi. (9.6 km) hike one way. They are certainly worth the effort, but the hike is very rigorous and certainly too much for a day trip. An overnight at Scott Clearing would put the cliffs within easier reach.

Trailhead: Turn south from NY 73 at a point 4.0 mi. (6.4 km) southeast of Lake Placid Village. There is a sign for the Adirondak Loj as well as a large DEC sign, "Trails to the High Peaks." Continue to the parking lot at the High Peaks Information Center (a daily parking fee is charged). Popularity of this trail access means parking is often highly competitive. No parking is allowed along the road. This facility and Adirondak Loj, just down the road, are owned by the Adirondack Mountain Club and maintained for the benefit of the hiking public as well as members of the club.

The trail to Indian Pass and Rocky Falls, starts to the west from the turnaround at the entrance station. The red marked trail follows an old road next to Heart Lake, turns right and passes the start of the trail to Mt. Jo. Continue straight to a trail register at 0.4 mi. (0.6 km). At 0.5 mi. (0.8 km) the Old Nye Ski Trail branches right. Stay left, passing the end of Heart Lake. Another ski trail turns left at the property line.

The trail is now pleasantly rolling, crossing brooks at 1.6 mi. (2.6 km) and at 2.1 mi. (3.4 km). Just past this second brook the loop trail to Rocky Falls branches right. This trail leads to Indian Pass Brook and up along the right side of the brook to a crossing to a lean-to. This is not a high waterfall, but there are lots of nice resting or picnic spots and a good swimming hole. This loop trail continues to ascend steeply to join the main Indian Pass trail. At the junction turn right to extend the hike toward Scott Clearing (1.4 mi. [2.2 km]) and Indian Pass (3.6 mi. [5.8 km]) or left to return to Heart Lake.

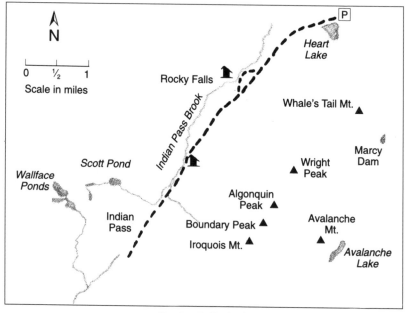

Rocky Falls (25)

26. Whiteface Landing and Lean-to

Round-trip to Whiteface Landing: 5.0 mi. (8.0 km)
Round-trip to lean-to: 7.2 mi. (11.5 km)
Elevation change: to Whiteface Landing, 190 ft.
 (58 m); to Whiteface lean-to, 400 ft. (122 m)
Map: Lake Placid 15' or Lake Placid metric

For older children not yet used to wearing a (lightly) loaded back-pack, this easy overnight hike is good practice for the bigger trips they may already be imagining. The site of the lean-to has a distinctly remote feel to it. As always, since one cannot count on the lean-to being unoccupied, bring a tent as an alternate shelter. In extremely buggy periods, a tent with mosquito netting closures may be the preferred choice in any case. Making Whiteface Landing the destination of a day hike, at 5.0 mi. (8.0 km) round-trip, is also an option.

Trailhead: On NY 86, 3.1 mi. (5.0 km) east of its junction with NY 73 in Lake Placid, and 0.2 mi. (0.3 km) west of a bridge over the West Branch of the Ausable River, a dirt road turns north. Drive down this road, bearing left at 0.5 mi. (0.8 km). A parking area marked with DEC signs is about 70 yd. (64 m) further along the road.

The trail continues on the road, bearing left where a private residence is seen on the right. It skirts the left shore of Connery Pond, and at 0.4 mi. (0.6 km) arrives at a gate. From here the trail is gently rolling still heading mainly north. At 2.5 mi. (4.0 km) a junction is reached. To the left a short walk leads to Whiteface Landing with a view down the length of Lake Placid, a nice lunch spot. Turning right the trail climbs gently to a straight section of old road at 3.1 mi. (5.0 km) with Whiteface Mountain in view directly ahead. In the next 0.5 mi. (0.8 km) the trail crosses Whiteface Brook three times, the final time just before reaching the lean-to at 3.6 mi. (5.8 km). Executing these crossings gracefully with a full pack may be a challenge.

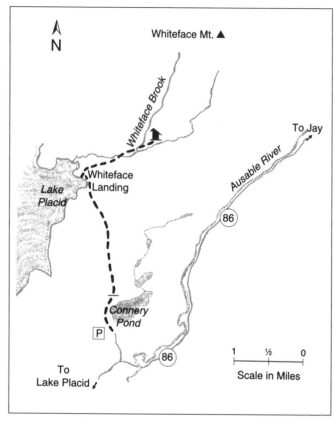

Whiteface Landing and Lean-to (26)

The trail up Whiteface Mountain from here is a steep 2.4 additional mi. (3.8 km). The elevation change from here would be 2800 ft. (853 m). If you decide to try it, the hike is likely to take more time than you would expect for that distance.

> *When planning an overnight trip with children it's important to be able to suggest activities to interest them until it's time for them to crawl into their sleeping bags. There may be short excursions nearby or the shore of a stream or pond to explore. Campsite setup, dinner preparation, and cleanup take time but may not engage the children. One adult may be in charge of camp duties while another reads or plays a game with the children.*

27. St. Regis Mountain

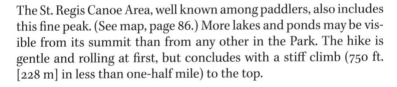

Round-trip: 6.8 mi. (10.9 km)
Elevation change: 1266 ft. (386 m)
Map: St. Regis 7.5', St. Regis 15', or St. Regis Mountain metric

The St. Regis Canoe Area, well known among paddlers, also includes this fine peak. (See map, page 86.) More lakes and ponds may be visible from its summit than from any other in the Park. The hike is gentle and rolling at first, but concludes with a stiff climb (750 ft. [228 m] in less than one-half mile) to the top.

Trailhead: At the junction of NY 86 and NY 30 in Paul Smiths, turn west on Keese Mills Road and drive 2.5 mi. (4.1 km) to a parking area on the left.

At the left side of the parking area, cross the bridge on foot and walk down the road 0.1 mi. (0.2 km) to the trailhead on the right. Sign in at the trail register and cross the plank footbridge, after which the trail turns left and climbs. This gently rolling trail passes through maple, yellow birch, hemlock, and balsam. At a height of land shortly before the trail climbs over a rocky bump, glance right to see a collection of very large rocks about 40 yd. off the trail. These enormous glacial erratics are certainly worth a short exploration.

The trail continues on a sidehill over roots and rocks, passing through a fine grove of hemlocks with views through the open understory. The trail now drops down off the ridge it has been following to reach a low point at 1.5 mi. (2.4 km). A long, straight, but gentle climb ensues, followed by a descent to join the old trail at 2.2 mi. (3.5 km). Just after crossing the bridge at this junction you will see a trail branch left to a campsite, where the cabin for the St. Regis fire tower observer once stood.

Now steeper, the main trail reaches sections that have been improved by recent maintenance work. Steady, steep climbing leads to the summit at 3.4 mi. (5.4 km). The top is mostly bare, attesting to a burn by surveyors in 1876. Following such treatment, the thin soil washes away and bare rock remains.

In all directions many peaks and lakes are in view, including the High Peaks to the southeast, the waters of the St. Regis Canoe Area to the immediate south, and the isolated peaks of Azure and Debar Mountains to the north.

28. Jenkins Mountain
Round-trip: 8.2 mi. (13.1 km)
Elevation change: 780 ft. (238 m)
Map: St. Regis 15' or St. Regis Mountain metric

This is a long, but not difficult, hike with many interesting sections. Hiking just to the end of the esker would be a worthwhile outing, shortening the round-trip to 6.0 mi. (9.6 km). The most interesting part of the hike is probably between the second and third mile. Inquire at the Visitor Interpretive Center (VIC) at Paul Smiths, where a trail map can be obtained as well as information on trail conditions.

Trailhead: Park in the Visitor Interpretive Center, 0.9 mi. (1.4 km) north of the intersection of NY 30 and NY 192 at Paul Smiths. The trail to Jenkins Mountain begins at the gazebo. Many other trails (see the section on Paul Smiths VIC), some wheelchair accessible, lace the lands surrounding the Visitor Center.

The trail begins along Barnum Brook, following the well-maintained trails and boardwalks. The trail to Jenkins Mountain continues northwest up the bank of Barnum Brook until it meets a dirt road. Go left on this road. From here the trail has mile markers every 0.5 mi. (0.8 km). Along this road you may see evidence of a silvaculture research project that is studying the effect of various forest clearing practices. Just before the 2.0-mi. (3.2-km) mark the road

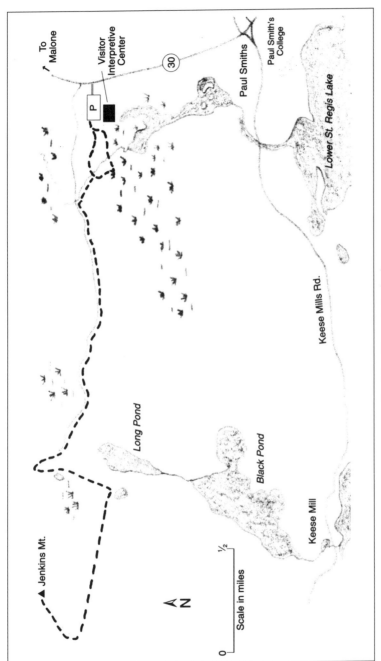

Jenkins Mountain (28)

narrows and continues as a trail heading south. From here the route gets more interesting. The cliffs of Jenkins Mountain are on the right and a footbridge passes a large beaver pond just below the impressive beaver dam.

The trail continues along the esker through lovely woods and past a fern-filled depression we called "Fern Gully." Between 2.5 mi. (4.0 km) and 3.0 mi. (4.8 km) some steep sections are encountered, and you may glimpse Long Pond down to the left. As the esker ends, the trail makes a sharp turn right, climbing gently toward Jenkins Mountain. At 3.0 mi. (4.8 km) the trail enters a hardwood forest, with open views through the beech, maple, and cherry trees. It follows this lovely valley heading west and nearly level until the trail bends to the north, then northeast, and climbs to the summit, with views of St. Regis Mountain and the High Peaks to the south.

The 8.2-mi. (13.1-km) round-trip makes this a long hike for young legs. We were lucky to find numerous attractions along the way. Beavers were active in the pond, including young ones playing as the adults worked. Toads, birds, and an incredible army of beetles provided frequent excitement. Bring plenty of water and insect repellent, and plan to picnic on the summit.

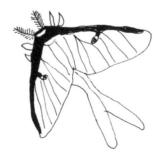

Keene, Keene Valley Section

The region that calls itself "Home of the High Peaks" is also attractive for its smaller peaks and wilderness camping spots. The mountains dominate this area. The lakes are small and the rivers narrow and fast moving. Access to this region is by NY 73 and NY 9N off the Adirondack Northway.

OTHER ATTRACTIONS IN THIS SECTION:

- Adirondack Center Museum, Elizabethtown (518-873-6466)
- Public Campgrounds (call 1-800-456-2267 for reservations)
  Lincoln Pond—south of Elizabethtown
  Sharp Bridge—US 9, north of North Hudson

29. Gulf Brook Lean-to and Lost Pond
Round-trip to the lean-to: 2.2 mi. (3.5 km)
Round-trip including Lost Pond: 3.6 mi.
  (5.8 km)
Elevation change: to Gulf Brook lean-to, 98 ft. (30 m);
  to Lost Pond, 605 ft. (185 m)
Map: Keene 7.5', Jay Mountain 7.5', and Rocky Ridge Peak 7.5';
  Lake Placid 15'; or Lewis metric

This is a nice first camping choice. (See map, page 101.) It's only a 1.1 mi. (1.8-km) walk along a fairly easy trail in good condition to the lean-to at the trail junctions to Hurricane Mountain and Lost Pond.

Trailhead: Turn east on the East Hill Road at the north end of the town of Keene and drive 2.3 mi. (3.7 km), then turn left onto O'Toole Road. This is a good dirt road until its final mile, which is marked "seasonal road." From here the road is steep and eroded and should be avoided in spring or extremely wet weather. The road ends in a large parking area. On the right is the trail to Gulf Brook lean-to and Hurricane Mountain.

The trail starts over a small wooden bridge at the southeast corner of the parking area. A small stream is crossed at 0.4 mi. (0.6 km). About halfway in on the left there is a large boulder with a split right down the middle. What could have done that? The lean-to at 1.1 mi. (1.8 km) is quite close to the brook—a sizable and noisy stream, with lots of small pools for bathing or playing.

Our original plan was to hike the 2.0-mi. (3.2-km) trail up Hurricane Mountain from the lean-to. This would probably be the easiest route up Hurricane, if done as an overnight. The elevation gain from the lean-to to the summit is less than 1500 ft. (457 m), but over only 2.0 mi. (3.2 km), which is steep going.

Instead, we followed the trail markers for the three-quarters-mile hike to Lost Pond, which has a nice setting with some rocky crags ringing it to the north. The trail can be muddy and there were some blowdown sections we had to go around. Another lean-to on the north end of Lost Pond could be the destination for a slightly longer, but not much more difficult, hike.

> *At the end of a long, hot day it feels good to dip down into a clear running stream and marvel at how cold Adirondack waters can be, even in late summer.*

30. Big Crow Mountain
    Round-trip: 1.4 mi. (2.2 km)
    Elevation change: 550 ft. (168 m)
    Map: Keene 7.5' and Jay Mountain 7.5', Ausable Forks 15',
        or Lewis metric

Some people say that on a clear day twenty-eight major peaks can be seen from the summit of Big Crow Mountain. This is the heart of the High Peaks area, and the prospect from the top is truly inspiring.

Trailhead: Turn east on the East Hill Road at the north end of the town of Keene and drive 2.3 mi. (3.7 km), then turn left onto O'Toole Road. This is a good dirt road until its final mile, which is marked "seasonal road." From here the road is steep and eroded and should be avoided in spring or extremely wet weather. The road ends in a large parking area. On the right is the trail to Gulf Brook lean-to and Hurricane Mountain. Ahead, at the north end, is the start of the trail to Big Crow Mountain.

The beginning of the trail has been cleared through an area of much

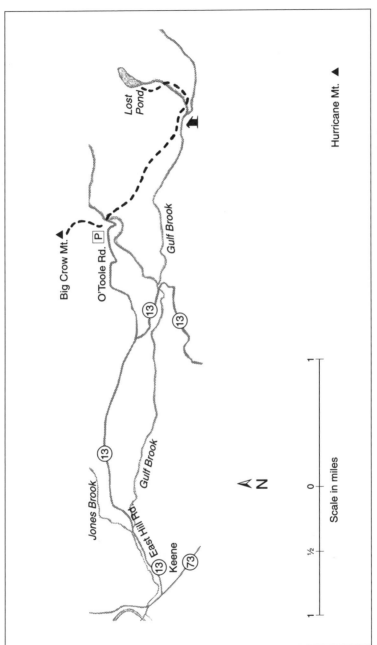

Gulf Brook Lean-to and Lost Pond (29) and Big Crow Mountain (30)

windfall. It is nearly level at first, passing through balsam and birch trees. Shortly after rock hopping over a small stream, the trail begins to climb. The ascent gets steeper just before a junction with the trail to Nun-da-ga-o Ridge to the right. A sign indicates 0.1 mi. (0.2 km) to Big Crow Mountain. A stiff rock scramble ends at the open rocky summit with good views in all directions. For such a short hike the sense of remoteness is surprising. It gives one of the best, and most underappreciated, views of the High Peaks, and is worth spending some time enjoying.

31. Baxter Mountain

   Round-trip: 2.2 mi. (3.5 km)
   Elevation change: 770 ft. (235 m)
   Map: Mt. Marcy 15' or Keene Valley metric

This is a short and mostly gentle hike to a good picnic spot with views of Keene Valley, the Great Range, and Mt. Marcy.

Trailhead: A sign marks the start of the trail on the south side of NY 9N, 2.0 mi. (3.2 km) east of the NY 9N-NY 73 intersection. Park along the side of the road.

 The trail begins gradually, crossing under power lines through second-growth pines. At about 0.2 mi. (0.3 km) the trail steepens, remaining wide and easy to follow. At 0.7 mi. (1.1 km), the trail from Beede Farm in Keene Valley joins the main trail from the left. The trail now begins a steep climb. Good views are frequent as the trail continues, ascents alternating with flat spots. At 0.9 mi. (1.4 km) the eastern summit is reached. A short dip and a rock scramble lead to the western summit at 1.1 mi. (1.8 km). Many paths wind through blueberry bushes between these points.

> *This is a fine first hike, with good views and picnic spots. It can be done easily in less than an hour. A three-year-old was lunching at the top when we were there.*

32. Pitchoff Mountain Lookout

Round-trip: 3.0 mi. (4.8 km)
Elevation change: 880 ft. (268 m)
Map: Keene Valley 7.5', or Mt. Marcy 15', or Keene Valley metric

On any fine day from spring to fall, you are sure to find company on this favorite lookout, especially on weekends. Ease of access, a short trail, fine views, and interesting balanced rocks all contribute to its popularity.

Trailhead: By far the most popular and shortest route to the lookout starts near the north end of Upper Cascade Lake, on NY 73, 4.5 mi. (7.2 km) east of the junction with Adirondak Loj Road. A sign marks the trailhead, and there is a parking lot, shared with the Cascade Mountain trail, directly across the highway.

The red DEC marked trail climbs steeply at first before turning easterly and becoming more gradual. At 0.8 mi. (1.3 km), the trail climbs again, reaching a small lookout on the right. A short distance on is a better lookout, with Cascade Lakes and Cascade Mountain in view.

The trail descends to a small saddle, then climbs several steep pitches. At 1.1 mi. (1.8 km) a former trail goes steeply right. Stay left and cross below some cliffs before swinging right and up to a junction at the top of the ridge (1.5 mi. [2.4 km]). This junction may not be obvious. The marked trail continues left, climbing another 0.5 mi. (0.8 km) along the ridge to the summit of Pitchoff (the ascent from highway is 1440 ft. [439 m]). The more popular destination is the lookout just 0.1 mi. (0.2 km) to the right from this junction. As you walk this short path, the surroundings suddenly change. You emerge from the low woods onto open rock to see two very large rocks balanced at the far edge of the cliff. It looks as if a good push could start them bounding downhill. Cascade Mountain, close at hand across the narrow valley, is only the most obvious of the many high peaks in view. This is a great place for a picnic lunch.

Our recent hike on Pitchoff brought home the importance of keeping a group together, even a small family group. At the junction with the abandoned trail at 1.1 mi. (1.8 km) we unwisely agreed to indulge one child in his desire to follow the steeper, older trail. One adult went with him, while the rest of the group

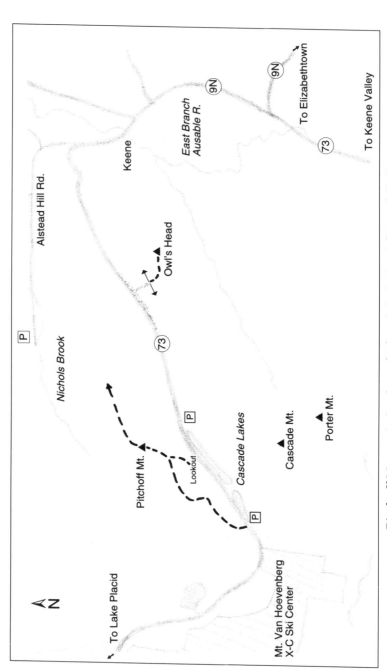

Pitchoff Mountain Lookout (32) and Owls Head (Keene) (34)

stayed on the main trail. We were only a few tenths of a mile from where the two paths were to rejoin, but we did not meet one another. The group on the main trail (without the guidebook) missed the turn heading towards the lookout and continued up towards the summit on the marked trail while the others waited at the lookout. We each thought the others were lost. We were reunited on the way down, but the anxiety of that experience taught us a lesson in trail togetherness. It led to a discussion with the boys on how to decide on the best options and what to do if you think someone in your party is lost.

33. Mt. Gilligan

Round-trip: 2.2 mi. (3.5 km)
Elevation change: 670 ft. (204 m)
Map: Rocky Ridge Peak 7.5' and Elizabethtown 7.5',
   Elizabethtown 15', or Elizabethtown metric

This short hike has some fine scrambling and offers good views of the Dix Range and Rocky Peak Ridge leading up to Giant Mountain. Steep pitches alternate nicely with flat spots and there are good views at several points on the climb.

Trailhead: On US 9, 3.6 mi. (5.8 km) north of its junction with NY 73, a dirt road leads east to a bridge over the Boquet River. There is a parking lot just before the bridge. Park here and cross the bridge on foot. Just before a garage, the trail, with ADK markers, heads into the woods on the left.

Flat for the first 0.2 mi. (0.3 km), the trail then turns right and climbs steeply. It becomes very steep, passing some rock walls before leveling out. It reaches a first lookout at 0.3 mi. (0.5 km). The trail now dips, then climbs past a large rounded boulder to another lookout at 0.6 mi. (1.0 km). It moves along a ridge before dropping to cross an old logging road, faint traces of which can be seen coming up from the right. Just beyond here it passes a large overhung rock on the right, and leads to a lookout at 0.9 mi. (1.4 km). This is a fine destination, but a higher lookout can be reached at 1.1 mi. (1.8 km).

Again and again we are amazed at the energy stores children can have. We contemplated this hike at the end of an already busy day. The boys were tired but game. Up the trail we went as they drove imaginary cars, having all sorts of "accidents" along the way. When we reached the overhung rock, they insisted it had to be explored. A game and a good mood can go a long way.

34. Owls Head (Keene)

Round-trip: 1.2 mi. (1.9 km)
Elevation change: 460 ft. (140 m)
Map: Owls Head 7.5', Lake Placid 15', or Keene Valley
   and Lake Placid metric

This is a small peak with big views. (See map, page 104.) Like its big brother, Cascade Mountain, just up the road, Owls Head sees lots of traffic go by every day. It is climbed by far fewer, though, which is too bad. This is an ideal hike for the young, and for others who may find climbing a high peak more effort than they can really enjoy. But be warned: it's a teaser. You keep thinking you've reached the top, only to find the trail goes up a bit farther.

Trailhead: A short dirt road leads south off NY 73, 3.2 mi. (5.1 km) west of Keene and 3.6 mi. (5.8 km) east of the trailhead for Cascade Mountain. A large wooden sign, "Owls Head Acres," marks the turn. Proceed on the dirt road approximately 0.2 mi. (0.3 km) to a junction. The trail is straight ahead and parking is available at the side of the road. The trail is on private land, but is easy to locate and follow.

The trail starts uphill immediately, but flattens somewhat within a few minutes. It is more eroded and rocky as more elevation is gained. At 0.3 mi. (0.5 km) the trail reaches an open ledge with good views to the west. A gentle climb through pines leads to another ledge with outlooks toward Pitchoff, Cascade, and the road winding between them. The trail proceeds east along a ridge, then ends with a rock scramble to the last "top" (0.6 mi. [1.0 km]). Some narrow spots near the top with sharp drops to the side call for caution. Continue ten minutes more along the ridge for a view east, including the valley connecting Keene and Keene Valley, and Baxter Mountain on its far side.

This little mountain has four (or more) "false summits." It offers the chance to say "we're at the top," when your small hikers have reached their limits. Some impressive cliffs, used for rock-climb-

ing instruction, are seen at the top, with a trail along their base.
At the start of the descent, take care over some steps that are big
for small legs.

35. Deer Brook and Snow Mountain

Round-trip loop through the flume and back: 1.4 mi.
   (2.2 km)
Round-trip to Snow Mountain: 3.4 mi. (5.4 km)
Elevation change: 500 ft. (152 m) to top of flume; 1360 ft.
   (415 m) to Snow Mountain summit
Map: Keene Valley 7.5', Mt. Marcy 15' or Keene Valley metric

This is not a beginner's hike. The walk up this flume (a deep, narrow
channel with a stream running through it) is challenging, but just
the kind of scrambling more experienced older children really enjoy.
The flume walk can be extended for a not-too-difficult ascent of
Snow Mountain. We recommend the flume walk during the drier
summer season, for experienced hikers who like to scramble.

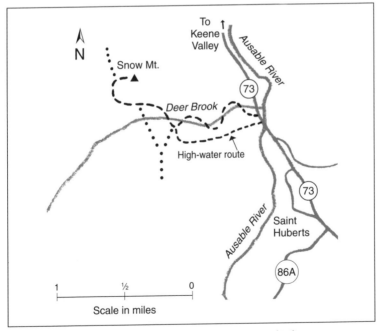

Deer Brook and Snow Mountain (35)

Trailhead: The hike starts on Rt. 73, 0.1 mi. (0.2 km) north of a bridge crossing the Ausable River, just north of St. Huberts. Parking is on the highway. An inconspicuous Adirondack Trail Improvement Society (ATIS) sign marks the trailhead; red ATIS disks mark the trail.

The trail leaves the traffic noises behind quickly, as the splashing brook becomes your companion for the next 0.7 mi. (1.1 km). Go up the left side of Deer Brook to a junction at a private driveway at 0.1 mi. (0.2 km). The Deer Brook trail continues straight ahead along the streambank. There's a small green sign here. The trail to the left follows a private driveway and is marked as the high-water route. It's closed to public vehicular traffic or parking and continues 0.6 mi. (1.0 km) to where the trail reenters the woods and joins the main trail at 0.7 mi. (1.1 km). This is the way to walk if the water runs high or if an easier ascent to Snow Mountain is desired.

The flume trail crosses and recrosses the brook many times, and is often quite steep and narrow as it winds through large boulders. The rock walls loom over the trail to spectacular effect. This may be the most picturesque short flume walk in the High Peaks area. After you cross the brook several times you are on the right side under an overhanging rock wall. There's a huge cave to the right. Your final crossing is here, to the left side of the brook. The trail climbs up and away from the brook. Within 100 yd. (91 m) it reaches a junction with the high-water route. The trail back to the highway via the high-water route goes to the left; a connecting trail to the W. A. White Trail from the Ausable Club goes straight ahead.

The trail to Snow Mountain continues right. Following this about 0.2 mi. (0.3 km) you reach a bridge over the brook. A sign directs you to an attractive waterfall three minutes up a spur trail on the right bank.

Snow Mountain is another 0.8 mi. (1.3 km) of moderate hiking. The trail crosses the bridge and follows a tote road at a moderate grade that eases off just before a junction at 1.3 mi. (2.1 km). Turning right, the trail continues on a flat in a beautiful open valley to a junction at 1.4 mi. (2.2 km). Turning right again, the Snow Trail proceeds across a side hill for a little over 100 yd. (91 m) and then turns right and ascends steeply to the first ledge at 1.6 mi. (2.6 km), from which there is a good view of Rooster Comb to the west. The trail reenters the woods and climbs to a second ledge. The summit is just beyond at 1.7 mi. (2.7 km). From its open rocky top there are views of Giant, Noonmark, Dix, and other High Peaks.

We recommend returning to the highway via the high-water route. Most of the way is along an unpaved driveway, but it is much easier than descending the flume. There are trail markers along the driveway and you will return to where you crossed the driveway on your way up the flume. The last 300 yd. (274 m) is again along the brook back to the highway.

Minerva, Newcomb Section

This is the heart of the Adirondacks. The Hudson River cuts through the mountains on its wild ride south. The country is rugged and still has a frontier feel in places. NY 28N climbs up over the spine of the mountains to drop down at the middle of lovely Long Lake. On the way it offers some of the best roadside views of the High Peaks.

OTHER ATTRACTIONS IN THIS SECTION:

- The Santanoni Preserve, Newcomb
- Barton Garnet Mine, North River; tours available (518-251-2706)
- Frontier Town, North Hudson (518-532-7181)
- Natural Stone Bridge and Caves, Pottersville (518-494-2283)
- Public Campgrounds (call 1-800-456-2267 for reservations)
    Harris Lake—Newcomb
    Lake Eaton—north of Long Lake
    Sharp Bridge—north of North Hudson

36. Visitor Interpretive Center at Newcomb
Round-trip: possibilities range from 0.6 mi. (1.0 km) to 1.2 mi. (1.9 km)
Elevation change: Minimal
Map: Newcomb 7.5', Newcomb 15', or Newcomb metric

Like the VIC at Paul Smiths, this site has some wonderful first hikes and is a good place to learn more about the Adirondacks. There is a very comfortable main building where educational programs are offered throughout the year. Call the Center for more specific information (518-582-2000).

The Center is located 1.4 mi. (2.2 km) west of the Newcomb Town Hall on NY 28N. There is a sign at the entrance on the north side of the road.

There are three marked trails at the Center. None of the trails is very difficult. Maps are available in the main building. A brief description of each is given below.

- **Rich Lake Trail**—0.6-mi. (1.0-km) loop. This trail skirts Rich Lake. It passes through cedar swamps, open hardwoods, and an old-growth hemlock forest. There are several places to sit along the way.

  - **Peninsula Trail**—0.9-mi. (1.4-km) loop (includes some of the Rich Lake Trail to take you to and from the Center). This trail follows the high rocky peninsula into Rich Lake. It leads through an old hemlock forest and crosses a pontoon bridge over a wetland area.

    - **Sucker Brook Trail**—0.8-mi. (1.3-km) loop. This trail follows the outlet of Rich Lake. It leads through cedar groves, across wetlands on boardwalks, to the site of a log dam. There's much beaver activity along this trail.

37. Boreas River Trail

Round-trip: 2.4 mi. (3.8 km)
Round-trip loop: 2.8 mi. (4.5 km)
Elevation change: Minimal
Map: Tahawus 7.5', Newcomb 15', or Newcomb metric

This is a loop trail comprising the Hewitt Eddy Trail and the Boreas River Trail. This easy 2.0-mi. (3.2-km) walk can be made into a loop by an 0.8-mi. (1.3-km) return along NY 28N to the starting point. If two or more adults are along, one adult could walk back for the car. If you would rather do an out and back, we recommend starting at the northern end, just south of the Boreas River bridge. Hike in as far as you like, or until the trail branches away from the river at Hewitt Eddy, then return to the start.

Trailhead: Access to the south trailhead is off the west side of NY 28N, 0.8 mi. (1.3 km) south of the Boreas River bridge. This is 7.9 mi. (12.6 km) north of Minerva and 6.5 mi. (10.4 km) south of the NY 28N intersection with Tahawus Road. A small DEC sign marks the trailhead. Park at the pull-off along the road.

The Hewitt Eddy Trail begins with a gentle descent from the NY 28N trailhead, with the smell of pine needles in the air. There is a 0.2-mi. (0.3-km) gradual ascent to a ridge with enormous pines and white birches. The trail narrows and you hear running water as you approach the right bank of Stony Pond Brook at 0.5 mi. (0.8 km). Leaving the brook, the trail heads north and reaches Hewitt Eddy, a wide point on the Boreas River. Going upstream from the eddy, you are now on the Boreas River Trail.

The Boreas River Trail stays close to the river for its entire length (1.2 mi. [1.9 km]). This section offers many beautiful spots to rest, picnic, or cool tired feet, legs, and more! The river is a series of cascades and small pools separated by quiet flows. Look for small places to explore and places where rocks permit you to get right onto the river. One rock, near the end of the walk, has an enormous metal ring in it from logging days. There are a few wet, muddy areas. Some trail sections are very close to the water; others climb above the water. You may want to keep a hand on a small toddler. The NY 28N bridge appears just before the trail emerges at the northern end.

The day we did this walk, during late August, we found so many examples of wonderful mushrooms we had never seen before that we nicknamed this walk the "Glorious Boreas, Humungus Fungus Walk." We decided to invest in a mushroom guide for future walks.

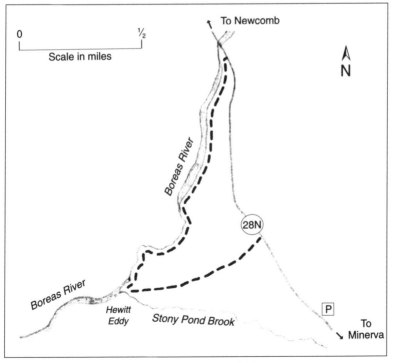

Boreas River Trail (37)

38. Stony Pond

Round-trip: 4.2 mi. (6.7 km)
Elevation change: Minimal
Map: Newcomb 15', Schroon Lake 15', or Dutton Mountain
    and Schroon Lake metric

This walk to a lovely pond is a nice picnicking destination or possible overnight camping opportunity.

Trailhead: The trailhead is on NY 28N, 3.9 mi. (6.2 km) north of the Olmstedville Road and NY 28N intersection in Minerva, or 2.8 mi. (4.5 km) south of the Hewitt Lake Club Road in Aiden Lair. There is a long pull-off area on the east side of the road. A DEC signpost marks the trailhead.

This woods road begins up a slight grade, but levels off quickly. At 0.3 mi. (0.5 km), a side trail to the right leads to an open campsite. A footpath descends 0.1 mi. (0.2 km) to the shore of Twentyninth Pond, of which the northern shoreline is state-owned.

A minor grade leads to a fork at 0.4 mi. (0.6 km). Bear left. From a height of land at 0.5 mi. (0.8 km), a long downgrade leads to a brook at 0.8 mi. (1.3 km). The trail continues to descend to cross Stony Pond Brook at a beaver dam at 1.0 mi. (1.6 km).

The trail now follows a valley. At 1.8 mi. (2.9 km) a final upgrade to Stony Pond begins. Stony Pond and its lean-to are reached at 2.1 mi. (3.4 km).

Holly Woodworth

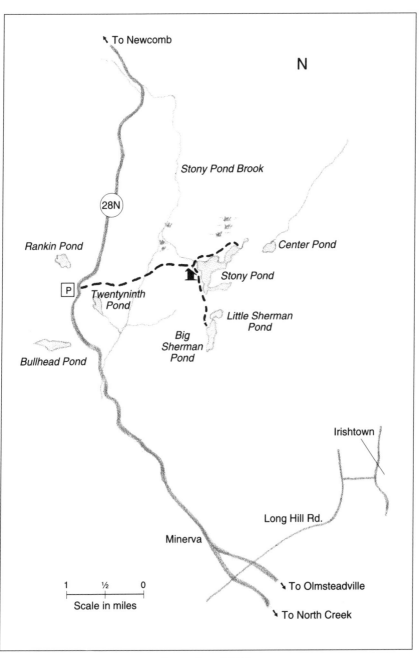

To Newcomb

N

Stony Pond Brook

28N

Rankin Pond

Center Pond

P

Stony Pond

Twentyninth Pond

Little Sherman Pond

Big Sherman Pond

Bullhead Pond

Irishtown

Long Hill Rd.

Minerva

1   ½   0

Scale in miles

To Olmsteadville

To North Creek

Stony Pond (38)

39. Goodnow Mountain

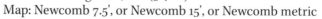

Round-trip: 3.8 mi. (6.1 km)
Elevation change: 1,040 ft. (317 m)
Map: Newcomb 7.5', or Newcomb 15', or Newcomb metric

This is a very well-maintained trail, part of the Archer and Anna Huntington Wildlife Forest Station of the College of Environmental Science and Forestry at Syracuse University. There's a fire tower at the top, as well as a ranger's building. Get a sense of the ranger's life by looking through the windows at the furnished room.

Trailhead: Access to the trail is on the south side of NY 28N, 1.5 mi. (2.4 km) west of the entrance to the Visitor Interpretive Center near Newcomb or 11.6 mi. (18.6 km) east of Long Lake Village. A large white sign marks the parking area. The trail, indicated by red markers with black arrows, begins to the left of the trail register. You may also find brochures here that give interesting information about the history and ecology of the forest, keyed to letters and numbers found along the trail.

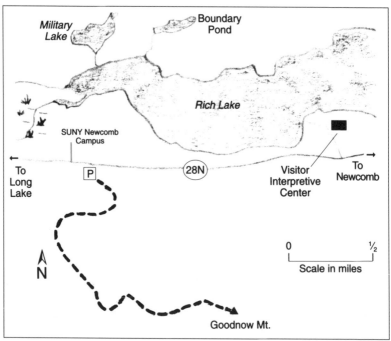

Goodnow Mountain (39)

The trail maintains a fairly steady ascent the whole way. There are many bridges over wet areas as well as benches that invite you to rest along the way. A small brook is passed at 0.5 mi. (0.8 km) and at 0.9 mi. (1.4 km) a ridge crest is reached. Bearing sharply left here, the trail winds its way through woods. You will notice cliffs on the right. At 1.5 mi. (2.4 km) a small side trail on the right takes you to a covered well, and then a small horse barn is seen on the right. The Huntingtons used to ride their horses to this point and then continue on foot to a small shelter farther on. Open rocks soon provide a good view to the right and in a few minutes you arrive at the rocky summit.

From the top of the fire tower, you can see twenty-three major peaks, including Marcy and Algonquin. There is fencing all around the stairs of the tower so it is a safe climb. A younger or fearful climber may appreciate your close presence while ascending. Even going up a few flights provides a good view. There is a small enclosed area at the top with a map to help locate some of the peaks.

Different hikes are remembered for different reasons. We found ourselves discussing trees a great deal on this hike. We identified a few trees by their bark or leaves and noticed the odd ways some of them grew. A good pastime for our children on the way down was counting bridges and benches. Which are there more of? The sibling penchant to turn anything into a contest sometimes has its uses. Water diversions could also have been added to the list of objects to count.

Blue Ledges (40)

40. Blue Ledges

Round-trip: 5.0 mi. (8.0 km)
Elevation change: Minimal
Map: Bad Luck Mountain 7.5' and Dutton Mountain 7.5',
   Newcomb 15', or Dutton Mountain metric

This could be a day hike or an overnight backpacking trip of medium difficulty. This is the only marked trail to a spot where the Hudson River makes a horseshoe bend at the base of gigantic 300-ft. (91-m) cliffs. It is a spectacular place.

Trailhead: Access to the trailhead is from the North Woods Club Road, off NY 28N 1.7 mi. (2.7 km) north of Minerva. This is 0.1 mi. (0.2 km) north of Minerva Hill Lodge. The North Woods Club Road forks west near the height of land on a curve. (If approaching from the south on NY 28N, it is easy to drive by without noticing it.) Pavement gives way to a narrow but generally smooth dirt road. After crossing the Boreas River, the D&H Railroad line is just beyond. The winding road climbs steeply up a grade. After a descent, a large DEC signpost on the south side of the road marks the trailhead, 6.7 mi. (10.7 km) from the highway. There is a large parking area on each side of the road.

The trail crosses a bridge at the east end of Huntley Pond then continues along the south shore of the pond for the first 0.3 mi. (0.5 km). It's a bit wet in spots, but nothing that cannot be addressed with good boots and moderate care in walking. The grades are gentle, with slightly increasing ascent as a height of land is reached at about 1.0 mi. (1.6 km). Soon thereafter the trail goes between two large boulders and begins to drop. The trail skirts the north side of a ridge, occasionally passing very large spruce, birch, and pine trees. It climbs gently again, turning south until the river can be heard below to the right. A small rocky outcrop is reached near some very impressive white pines. From here the descent to the river is more or less continuous, but never steep. The river is reached at a sandy bank, with a sign pointing left toward camping areas (about 0.1 mi. [0.2 km]).

The three campsites, each large enough for two backpacking tents, are easily found. It is fun to hop the rocks farther south along the river, which is noisy with rapids. Care is always needed, and this trip may not be advisable during high water in the spring.

The cliffs across the river are impressive, as are the trees which doggedly hang onto the extremely steep slopes. Rapids are found downstream. Just upriver, swimming holes offer a refreshing end to a hike done during the lower water of summer.

> *We had hoped to spy some kayakers or rafters along this stretch of the river, but it was probably too late in the season. The view whet our appetites for a future water trip along the Hudson. One of the nice things about the Adirondack Park is that it can be explored in many ways.*

Old Forge, Long Lake & Blue Mountain Section

The southwestern Adirondacks may not have the craggy peaks of the other sections, but the hiking and camping possibilities are numerous and delightful. The views over the rolling hills show lakes in nearly every pocket. Blue Mountain stands out from almost every vantage point in the area. Historical interest is well served by the outstanding Adirondack Museum in Blue Mountain Lake. Old Forge is also a center of interest and entertainment for vacationers.

OTHER ATTRACTIONS IN THIS SECTION:

- Great Camp Sagamore, Raquette Lake (315-354-5311)
- Arts Center, Old Forge (315-369-6411)
- Adirondack Museum, Blue Mountain Lake (518-352-7311)
- Adirondack Lakes Center for the Arts, Blue Mountain Lake (518-352-7715)
- McCauley Mountain Chairlift Ride, Old Forge (315-369-3225)
- Enchanted Forest/Water Safari, Old Forge; a water theme park (315-369-6145)
- Adirondack Scenic Railroad, NY 28, Thendara (315-369-6290)
- Public campgrounds (call 1-800-456-2267 for reservations)

    Brown's Tract Pond—west of Raquette Lake
    Eighth Lake—on NY 28
    Golden Beach—on Raquette Lake
    Lake Durant—east of Blue Mountain Lake
    Limekiln Lake—south of Inlet
    Little Sand Point, Point Comfort,
        and Poplar Point—all on Piseco Lake
    Nicks Lake—near Old Forge

41. Rocky Mountain

Round-trip: 1.0 mi. (1.6 km)
Elevation change: 440 ft. (134 m)
Map: Big Moose 15' or Eagle Bay metric

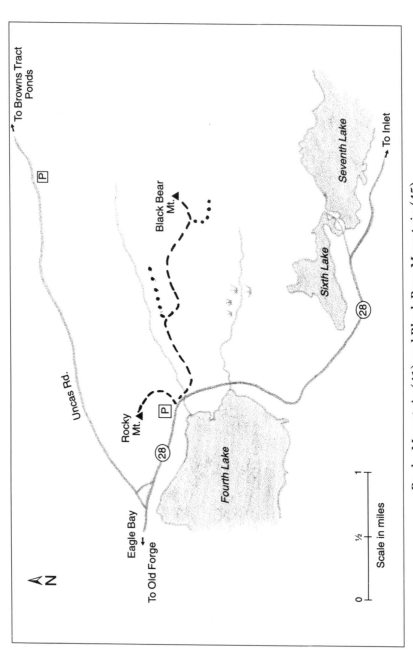

Rocky Mountain (41) and Black Bear Mountain (45)

This is a popular hike right off NY 28 that climbs to ledges overlooking Fourth Lake. With this short but steadily steep climb, the very young hiker will have a real feeling of accomplishment when he or she reaches the top.

Trailhead: From the junction of NY 28 and Big Moose Road in Eagle Bay, drive 1.2 mi. (1.9 km) east on NY 28. There is an extensive parking area on the left. From the opposite direction drive 0.9 mi. (1.4 km) toward Eagle Bay on NY 28 from the public parking area in the center of Inlet. The trailhead parking area will be on your right.

The trail begins at the center of the parking area. There is no sign. (The southeast end of the parking area is the start of the Black Bear Mountain Trail). The trail begins in a north-northeast direction but soon turns left. The wide, eroded trail is very easy to follow. The cliff top has a southwest drop-off with a wide open view of Fourth Lake and the village of Inlet. The open rocky sides of Bald Mountain are seen to the southwest. With sharp eyes or binoculars you may discern the fire tower on Bald Mountain. Very young hikers would enjoy the cars that look like toys moving along the ribbon of highway.

42. Bald (Rondaxe) Mountain

Round-trip: 2.0 mi. (3.2 km)
Elevation change: 390 ft. (119 m)
Map: Old Forge 7.5', Old Forge 15', or Old Forge metric

This is a very popular hike in the Old Forge area and one can easily see why. There's easy access to the trailhead, a nice short walk through the woods, and an open rock ridge at the top with great views. There is a fire tower at the top, but it is no longer climbable.

Trailhead: From the Tourist Information Center in Old Forge, drive 4.5 mi. (7.2 km) northeast on NY 28, turn left (northwest) on Rondaxe Road. In 0.2 mi. (0.3 km), park in the large area on the left. If coming from the village of Eagle Bay, at the junction of NY 28 and Big Moose Road, drive 4.5 mi. (7.2 km) west and southwest on NY 28 and then turn right on Rondaxe Road. There are trail signs and a register at the trailhead. The trail is marked with red DEC trail markers.

This is a heavily used trail with moderate grades. A large part of the ascent is on bedrock. It is a pleasant walk through deciduous forest, which soon becomes a spruce-fir forest. At 0.4 mi. (0.6 km) there are fine views of Second, Third, and Fourth Lakes. The final 600 ft. (183 m) to the fire tower is along a rocky ridge with fine views. First Lake comes into view as well as Blue Mountain to the east-north-east. Continuing along the ridge southwest past the fire tower, the trail reaches a boulder on a sloping ledge near the drop-off. It's fun to imagine how many people it would take to release it down the slope. One may continue along the ridge for quite a distance, so there is plenty of room for the throngs of people that climb this peak on nice weekends.

> *Despite efforts to give this peak a unique name, Bald Mountain it remains in local usage and on most signs and maps. Attempts to avoid proliferation of certain popular names in the Adirondacks have had only limited success, as anyone noting the number of Owls Head, Panther, Bear, and other (often animal) names will agree. One game we play is to see how many different animals are represented in Adirondack place names.*

43. Cascade Lake (Eagle Bay)

Round-trip: 3.2 mi. (5.1 km)
Elevation change: Minimal
Map: Eagle Bay 7.5', Big Moose 15', or Eagle Bay metric

The north shore of Cascade Lake was a girls' camp into the early decades of this century. Signs of the camp still remain. The most obvious vestiges are the woods road the trail follows and the large open area where the main camp buildings used to stand. The open area is now a popular and very attractive camping spot, and the sandy lake shore adds to its appeal. This is an excellent first camping choice as well as a day-trip destination. Use the designated camping areas. An outhouse is located nearby.

Trailhead: From NY 28 in Eagle Bay, turn northwest on Big Moose Road and drive just over 1.0 mi. (1.6 km). The first of two parking areas is on the right at a bend in the road. A sign there directs you 0.4 mi. (0.6 km) ahead to a larger parking area. Either may be used, as the trails converge at a large wooden trail map and trail register. It is a somewhat shorter walk from the first parking area.

From the register, the trail is an easy walk on an old road 0.8 mi. (1.3 km) east to a junction with the loop trail around Cascade Lake. Stay to the left, descending slightly and pass a spring on the right. At 0.9 mi. (1.4 km) the trail crosses the edge of a field and then the outlet of Cascade Lake on a short bridge. At 1.1 mi. (1.8 km) the red marked Cascade Lake Link Trail goes left. Continue straight. The trail bends toward the east and soon reaches the north shore of Cascade Lake. An outhouse can be seen on the left at 1.6 mi. (2.6 km) and shortly thereafter the camping area beneath larger white pine trees. A nice sand and gravel beach completes the picture.

Beyond the camping area the trail continues, passing several more campsites. Following this trail another 1.2 mi. (1.9 km) you reach the narrow, high waterfall that gives the lake its name. This would be a good additional hike for those whose energy levels have rebounded following a rest at the campsite.

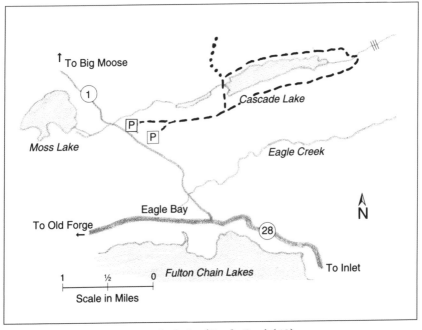

Cascade Lake (Eagle Bay) (43)

The seven-, ten-, and twelve-year-old children of one family had such a great experience wilderness camping in the Middle Settlement Lake area in this section of the Park that the children asked their parents to sell the pop-up camper and use the money to add to the family's backpacking gear. It's great when the desire for a wilderness hiking experience comes from the children.

44. Cascade Pond

Round-trip: 5.6 mi. (9.0 km)
Elevation change: Minimal
Map: Blue Mountain 7.5', Blue Mountain 15',
   or Blue Mountain Lake metric

Once we knew our children were capable of hiking several miles with their frame packs, we didn't think this hike would be too difficult. The walk in is fairly long but the pond is lovely.

Trailhead: Drive east on NY 28/30 from the NY 28/30/28N intersection in Blue Mountain Lake Village. At 0.9 mi. (1.4 km) from the intersection turn right onto Durant Road. Travel 0.2 mi. (0.3 km) to the small trailhead sign on the left at a narrow dirt road just before a cemetery. Parking is a short way down this road.

From the parking area, an arrow on a small sign points to an abrupt turn to the right. The path heads west. There were several muddy sections on the trail but all were easily negotiated. At 0.6 mi. (1.0 km) a small downhill leads to a 200-ft. (91-m) bridge across Rock Pond. This makes a nice rest stop and provides some relief if mosquitoes are a problem. The trail turns left at the end of the bridge and climbs a short ridge. It then descends steeply to a valley floor. It's a nice stroll through a hardwood forest with plenty of ferns. The trail narrows as it approaches Cascade Pond. The lean-to is reached at 2.8 mi. (4.5 km). There's a great view of the pond. There are also several nice tent sites before the lean-to. Head a short way back down the trail looking for well-worn paths toward the pond.

   For an alternative return route that makes this hike a loop of 6.4 mi. (10.2 km), continue past the lean-to on the trail that leads to Lake Durant Public Campground. In 0.9 mi. (1.4 km) you come to a junction with the Northville-Placid Trail. The trail to the Stephens Pond lean-to leads 0.6 mi. (1.0 km) to the right. Going left you will follow the wide and heavily used Northville-Placid Trail for 2.7 mi. (4.3 km). It's a gradual downhill that eventually takes you to the Lake Durant Public Campground. You will come out at campsite 3. Turn right onto the campground's truck road and work your way to the main entrance. It's about 3.0 mi. (4.8 km) back to the start along NY 28/30. If you plan to do this in reverse or to leave a second car, there is a large DEC sign to indicate where the Northville-Placid Trail crosses the highway (2.6 mi. [4.2 km] south on NY 28/30, east of Blue Mountain Lake). You can park here and avoid paying the day use fee charged to drive into the campground.

Halfway out on the second day it started to rain. It was a warm day and we were close to the end. We decided to skip the rain gear since we had extra clothes in the car. We listened to the rain hit the trees in the leafy cover above us, but it wasn't until about twenty minutes later that we felt any drops hit us!

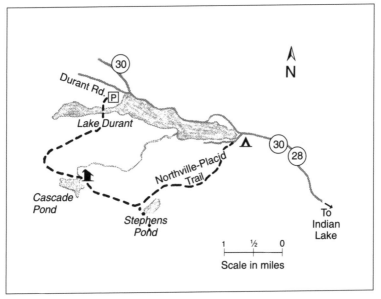

Cascade Pond (44)

45. Black Bear Mountain
Round-trip: 3.8 mi. (6.1 km)
Elevation change: 728 ft. (222 m)
Map: Eagle Bay 7.5', Big Moose 15', or Eagle Bay metric

This is a scenic mountain with great views from the open rock on the southeast side of the crest. (See map, page 122.) The mountain may have gotten its name from the blackened rocks and trunks that crowned the top after numerous fires early in the century or possibly because so many bears were attracted to the berries that grew there after the fires. Once the property of the financier J. Pierpont Morgan, this has long been a favorite place to hike for visitors and residents alike. There are several routes up this mountain. We have chosen the most popular and direct route.

Trailhead: From the junction of NY 28 and Big Moose Road in Eagle Bay, drive 1.2 mi. (1.9 km) east on NY 28. There is an extensive parking area on the left. From the opposite direction drive 0.9 mi. (1.4 km) toward Eagle Bay on NY 28 from the public parking area in the center of Inlet and the trailhead parking will be on your right. The trail begins at the end of the pavement at the southeast end of the parking area (toward Inlet).

From the southeast end of the parking area, walk 50 yd. (46 m) to the trail sign. The sign indicates this is a snowmobile trail and there are yellow DEC markers. Turn left onto the beginning of a woods road, and pass a barrier across it in another 30 yd. (27 m). The route continues east on a woods road with a stream to the left.

At 0.7 mi. (1.1 km) there is a grassy clearing. Here the blue route, which you will follow, goes off towards the right. It is the more obvious trail. The grassy trail to the left, used by skiers, is a much longer and more difficult route to follow. The blue route is an old logging road that climbs to a nearly level clearing at 0.9 mi. (1.4 km). Beyond the clearing the old road curves left and continues on level ground as an open, grassy, but often wet, route.

At 1.1 mi. (1.8 km) the route enters the woods. The climbing is gradual here. At 1.7 mi. (2.7 km) a steep ascent begins on a rocky and rooted trail. Though the trail has been cleared, there is much evidence of recent high winds in the large trunks tumbled about, with great root masses jutting as much as ten feet into the air. Continuing steeply, at 1.8 mi. (2.9 km) a privately maintained red blazed trail enters from the right. The remainder of the ascent is mainly on rock with many of the sections requiring some scrambling. The trail reaches the open rock ledge summit at 1.9 mi. (3.0 km). There are views of Seventh Lake and on very clear days some of the high peaks can be seen on the far horizon above Raquette Lake. Mt. Marcy appears to the left of prominent Blue Mountain. This is a wonderful summit for basking on the many rocky knobs in the warmth of a sunny day while enjoying a picnic lunch. To the north is the large Pigeon Lake Wilderness Area, but the best views are to the south. In season, you are sure to see boat traffic or even float planes on the busy Fulton Chain Lake below.

> *High winds can be dangerous anywhere, but especially so in the forest. Storms like the July 1995 "microburst," which felled many large trees, are uncommon, but any winds can bring down limbs or even whole trees. Sometimes one tree stops the fall of another, or causes another to split. Sometimes limbs hang precariously above the trail, so we scoot by, and sometimes a ducking challenge is offered. Children enjoy looking for evidence of destruction by wind or lightning. A fallen trunk may be tempting to climb on, especially if it crosses the trail, but make sure trunks and limbs won't break or fall, aren't too slippery, and that your child's exploring is safe.*

46. Castle Rock

Round-trip: 4.0 mi. (6.4 km)
Elevation change: 640 ft. (195 m)
Map: Blue Mountain 15' or Blue Mountain Lake metric

This hike offers expansive views over Blue Mountain Lake from a jagged rock peak rising above its north shore. This is the epitome of Adirondack lakes. Island-spangled Blue Mountain Lake has been much photographed and admired. Another fine view of it is from the Adirondack Museum at its northeast end.

Trailhead: Access is off NY 30/28N. Turn left onto Maple Lodge Road, 0.6 mi. (1.0 km) north of the NY 30/28N intersection in Blue Mountain Lake Village. There is a sign for Minnowbrook Conference Center. Drive 1.3 mi. (2.1 km) along a paved and then gravel road to the DEC trailhead sign for Upper Sargent Pond. Park beside the road at the entrance to the conference center. This is a private road. Be sure not to obstruct traffic.

Walk along the road from where you've left your car. Within 0.2 mi. (0.3 km) the road forks. Take the right fork. In another 0.2 mi. (0.3 km) the trail leaves the road to the right, heading uphill with a brook on the left. Follow DEC red markers. Enter the woods and begin to cross the first of the many small streams encountered in the next half mile. It will be a wet trail if the weather has been rainy. The trail passes east of Chub Pond at 0.7 mi. (1.1 km) and then generally swings west.

A small clearing is sighted on the left shortly before a sign notes the yellow marked trail to Castle Rock going left. Now elevation is gained, quickly at times. The trail reaches some large rock faces and angles up through narrow rock-walled places until a sharp turn right leads to a ledge and sudden, spectacular views south and east. Boats will usually be seen, wending their tiny ways among the many islands. Watch children closely; the ledge drops off sharply.

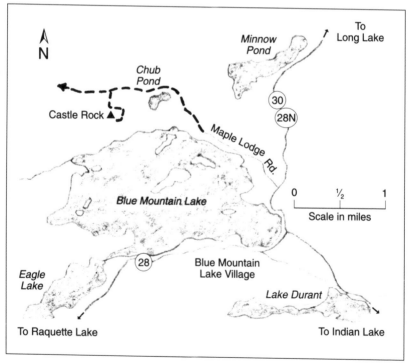

Castle Rock (46)

The rewards along the way are modest, especially in contrast to the vista that bursts forth at the end. It is, in some ways, an exercise in deferred gratification. To the east, Blue Mountain rises to lofty dominance over the entire area.

Another very rewarding spectacle is worth a short side-trip on the way back. Caves and recesses under the very rocks you have been standing on at the top can be reached back down the trail by way of a red blazed trail going left, just after you have passed the rock faces. A few hundred yards along this trail brings you to the first of these impressive spots. Return to the main trail for the descent.

> *Exuberant cries of "What a view!" burst forth as we came onto the open rock ledge. The added bonus of finding spotted newt efts among the recesses at the base of the rocks on the way down made this a very satisfying outing.*

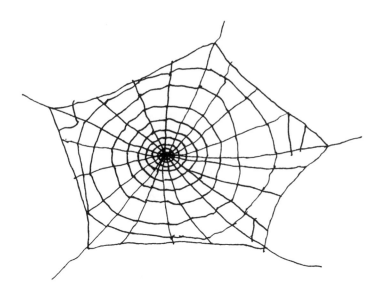

Indian Lake & South Section

The mountains do not rise high here, but the land is so rugged that it has resisted most attempts to tame it. Hiking and camping opportunities are excellent, especially for beginners. Numerous snowmobile trails add to the network of hiking possibilities.

OTHER ATTRACTIONS IN THIS SECTION:

- Sherman's Carousel, Caroga Lake; old merry-go-round and beach (518-835-4110)
- Public Campgrounds (call 1-800-456-2267 for reservations)
  Caroga Lake—NY 29A Gloversville
  Indian Lake Islands
  Lewey Lake—north of Speculator
  Moffit Beach—NY 8 west of Speculator
  Northampton Beach—NY 30 south of Northville
  Sacandaga—NY 30 south of Wells

47. Auger Falls

Round-trip: 1.0 mi. (1.6 km)
Round-trip loop: 1.3 mi. (2.1 km)
Elevation change: Minimal
Map: Wells 7.5', Lake Pleasant 15', or Bakers Mills metric

NY 30 parallels the Sacandaga River from Northville to Speculator. Much of the route is very scenic, especially on the southern portion where the river is broad and the road often quite close to it. In the northern portion, the river is narrower, and less often in view, but Auger Falls is well worth the short walk. It illustrates vividly the difference between the upper reaches of a river, as it drops rapidly from higher elevations, and its lower course, as it widens and slows its pace.

Trailhead: Just north of Wells, NY 30 and NY 8 join. At 1.7 mi. (2.7 km) north of this junction a dirt road on the right (east) leads to a large parking area. Park at the near end and walk south 0.1 mi. (0.2 km) on a short dirt road that parallels the main highway.

Look for a marked trail leading into the woods on the left. This short, mainly level trail, reaches the Sacandaga at a narrow gorge through which water tumbles noisily at 0.4 mi. (0.6 km). The walls of the gorge are steep and care should be taken to keep back. Keep a firm hand on toddlers. An unmarked but obvious path, which follows the river upstream, can be followed to complete a loop back to the other end of the parking area. It is heavily clogged by windfall at this writing (1997), but older children may enjoy the challenge of climbing over and under trunks and branches.

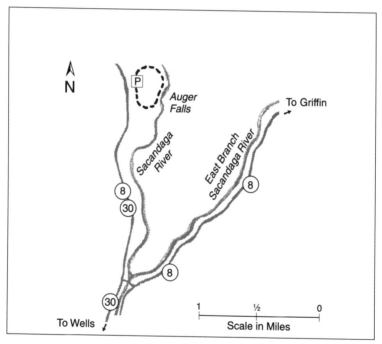

Auger Falls (47)

48. Tenant Creek Falls

Round-trip to the first falls: 1.8 mi. (2.9 km)
Elevation change: Minimal
Map: Harrisburg 15' or Hope Falls metric

The first of three lovely falls on Tenant Creek is reached by an easy well-marked trail. Another 1.0 mi. (1.6 km) along an increasingly faint footpath leads to the two upper falls. The beautiful basin at the foot of the first falls is more than enough reason to do this hike.

Trailhead: From the north, turn left on Creek Road, 8.5 mi. (13.6 km) south of the town of Wells. In about 2.0 mi. (3.2 km) bear left onto Hope Falls Road. Continue to the end of this road, bearing left at each of the two Y's. The final 1.5 mi. (2.4 km) of road is dirt. If approaching from the south, turn right onto Old Northville Road 0.5 mi. (0.8 km) after crossing the bridge over East Stony Creek on NY 30, just north of Northville. Go 1.5 mi. (2.4 km), then turn left at East Stony Creek Road and continue on it through the intersection with Creek Road (from the west).

The trail heads north along the right bank of East Stony Creek. The sign identifies it as the trail to Wilcox Lake. A trail register is soon passed on the right. Just before the trail crosses a large snowmobile bridge at 0.2 mi. (0.3 km), the trail to Tenant Creek Falls turns right, staying on the right bank of Tenant Creek. Yellow markers show the way through a grove of large hemlock trees. The trail is easy, at times climbing away from and above the creek. At 0.9 mi. (1.4 km) it drops to the large pool at the base of the falls. A bench and numerous rock ledges invite a long rest at this peaceful spot. Above the falls are several more cascades through large boulders. These would also be great picnic sites. The unmarked trail to the upper falls stays on the right bank of the creek, but becomes faint and harder to follow in its upper reaches.

49. Rock Lake

Round-trip: 1.6 mi. (2.6 km)
Elevation change: Minimal
Map: Blue Mountain 15' or Blue Mountain Lake metric

As a first "backcountry" camping trip, this spot is ideal. It is a short, flat walk in from the road, with several nice camping sites on the lake, but no lean-to. The view of Blue Mountain reflected in the water is splendid. Sawyer Mountain is just east of the trailhead for Rock Lake on NY 28. The two sites make a good combination for hiking and camping.

Trailhead: The parking area for Rock Lake is 5.0 mi. (8.0 km) east of the intersection on NY 30 and NY 28 in Blue Mountain Lake, and 1.6 mi. (2.6 km) west of the Sawyer Mountain trailhead. Don't take the trail 1.4 mi. (2.2 km) farther to the east, which also leads to Rock Lake, but then continues on to Rock River.

The well-marked western trail approaches Johnny Mack Brook at 0.3 mi. (0.5 km) and follows it to the lake, which is very marshy at this point. The trail crosses a bridge to the right just before reaching the lake. Shortly thereafter a path left leads toward a camping area, about 0.8 mi. (1.3 km) from the road.

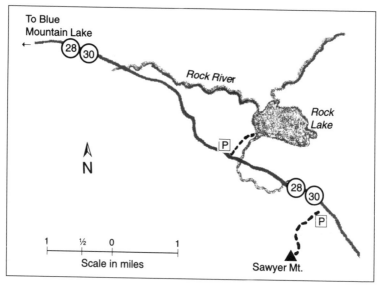

Rock Lake (49)

Twenty minutes has brought you to a spot that feels remote, and offers an impressive view of a major peak. There are said to be some fine camping areas on the northeast shore of the lake, but that's another mile-and-a-half farther east to join the Rock River trail, then north. Look for paths leading west to head to these camping spots.

50. Cod Pond

Round-trip: 2.4 mi. (3.8 km)
Elevation change: 150 ft. (50 m)
Map: South Mountain 7.5'

This is a popular spot for camping, picnicking and fishing. The location of Cod Pond also makes wildlife viewing an excellent possibility here.

Trailhead: Drive 9.5 mi. east on NY 8 from the point at which it diverges from NY 30 north of the village of Wells. Just before crossing the bridge over Stewart Creek there is a parking area on the right sufficient for 4–5 cars.

An unmarked path leads south from the parking area for about 500 ft. Here it joins a marked snowmobile trail. Continuing to climb, the trail comes to an intersection at 0.2 mi. (0.3 km). Turn right and continue to another junction at 0.4 mi. (0.6 km) where the Cod Pond Trail branches left. The walking becomes more level, until it climbs up a small ridge at 0.9 mi. (1.5 km). At 1.2 mi. (1.9 km) the trail reaches a large camping area, just beyond the shore of Cod Pond.

> *A friend who was several months pregnant joined us on one memorable hike. She may now entertain her son with the story of the mountain he climbed before he was born. Our boys find these tales fascinating because they seem to prove you can't be too young to enjoy hiking.*

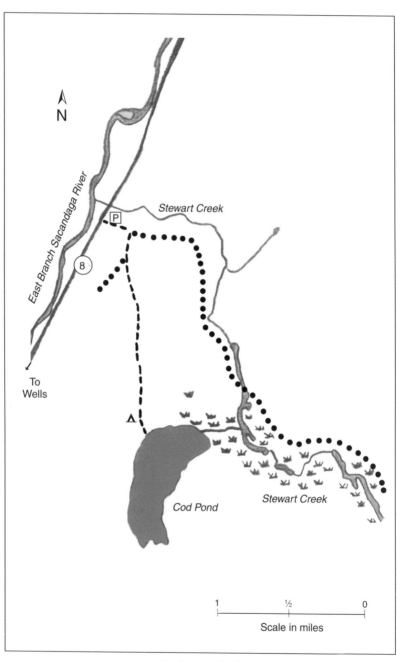

Cod Pond (50)

51. Echo Cliffs (Overlook on Panther Mountain)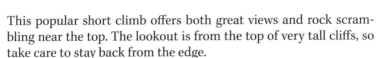
Round-trip: 1.5 mi. (2.4 km)
Elevation change: 680 ft. (207 m)
Map: Piseco Lake 7.5', Piseco Lake 15', or Piseco Lake metric

This popular short climb offers both great views and rock scrambling near the top. The lookout is from the top of very tall cliffs, so take care to stay back from the edge.

Trailhead: The trail goes north from the West Shore Road along Piseco Lake, 0.5 mi. (0.8 km) west of Little Sand Point State Campground. A DEC sign marks the start and blue trail markers are frequent.

The first part of the hike is fairly easy, though badly eroded in places, and it can be wet in spots. At 0.3 mi. (0.5 km) the trail levels off briefly. Most Adirondack trails regularly pass solitary boulders, either glacial erratics or pieces shed from weathering cliffs. This trail is populated with many, including some with very rectangular shapes. Watch for them through the trees. At 0.6 mi. (1.0 km) a large boulder appears on the left, looking from below like a gigantic cube. Just beyond is a lounge-chair-shaped rock that must be tested for comfort.

The trail gets quite a bit steeper as it moves past a large rock wall on the left. This marks the approach to the top, a boulder-studded set of outlooks with fine views of Piseco Lake, Spy Lake beyond to the southeast, and many hills in a 180-degree view to the south. The top offers some boulders and small chimneys that can be clambered up with care, but beware of the obvious danger points.

> *There's something special about a hike done late in the day, as was our climb here. Shadows were lengthening. The rocks were still warm from a day of sun. We'd set up camp at one of the three state campgrounds along the road, and the prospect of dinner at a campfire and a night in the tent added to the enthusiasm and energy of our little hikers.*

52. Sawyer Mountain

Round-trip: 2.2 mi. (3.5 km)
Elevation change: 650 ft. (198 m)
Map: Rock Lake 7.5', Blue Mountain 15',
   or Blue Mountain Lake metric

This easy climb was one of the first both our children hiked on their own two feet. The vistas from the top rewarded their efforts.

Trailhead: Travel east of Blue Mountain Lake Village on NY 28/30 for 6.0 mi. (9.6 km) to a parking area on the right side of the road.

The yellow-marked trail begins gently but soon becomes a moderate climb. Red paint blazes are interspersed with trail markers. At 0.9 mi. (1.4 km) the trail passes a large boulder on the right and, following a short level stretch, leads to a lookout to the east. The trail now crosses bare rock, but cuts quickly right, reentering the woods. The summit is wooded, but the trail continues 270 ft. (82 m) past the summit to an excellent lookout. In the far distance, Blue Mountain stands out boldly on the horizon. Sprague Pond is in front. Looking due west, narrow Stephens Pond is seen high up on Blue Ridge. The Northville-Placid Trail skirts this pond as it winds 133 miles through the Adirondacks. One of the most ambitious goals for Adirondack hikers is to walk the complete length of this trail. It is so popular that a separate guidebook has been written for the trail (see Selected References).

> *The boys never tired of saying, "I saw yer mountain!" as we descended from this peak. We saw some snakes sunbathing on top. Rocky outcrops are a favored habitat for snakes, most of which are not dangerous. The only region of the Adirondacks known to harbor poisonous snakes is the Lake George area.*

53. Kane Mountain

Round-trip: 1.8 mi. (2.9 km)
Elevation change: 600 ft. (183 m)
Map: Canada Lake 7.5'

Fine views from the fire tower on Kane Mountain and the several trails to its summit make this a popular small peak. We describe the

East Trail to the summit here. There is also an abandoned observer's cabin on top, which has been rehabilitated by the Canada Lake Protective Association and DEC.

Trailhead: Turn north where NY 10 passes between Canada Lake and Green Lake onto Green Lake Road. Drive 0.6 mi. (1.0 km) to the point at which a smaller dirt road to the trailhead branches left. Drive 200 yd. (183 m) down this road to a parking area. The red-marked DEC trail heads left from the parking area.

This trail benefits from the considerable maintenance work involved in building water bars at frequent intervals. A few wet spots remain, but it is mainly an easy, though moderately steep, hike. The trail begins to level out as it approaches the summit. A sharp eye will spot the girders of the fire tower through the trees. On busier weekends, expect to hear the sounds of other hikers. Views are only to be had from the tower. Pine Lake and West Canada Lake are seen nearby, with peaks in the Catskills visible on exceptionally clear days. Be sure to sign the summit register. Returning, take care to retrace your steps, following the East Trail, rather than the North or South Trails.

> *On our way up this mountain we noticed a family descending with an infant in a stroller! The dad was having a bit of a struggle with it and was carrying the stroller when we saw him. Adirondack trails are not easy places for strollers. There are better ways to carry infants which are more comfortable for both infant and parents (see Special Considerations for Infants and Toddlers).*

54. Good Luck Cliffs

Round-trip: 5.0 mi. (8.0 km)
Elevation change: 620 ft. (189 m)
Map: Canada Lake 7.5', Piseco Lake 15', or Morehouse
    Mountain and Honnedaga Lake metric

The final two-fifths of this hike is on an unmarked, but well-used path. With moderate care the way is easy to follow, and well worth the effort. An optional bushwhack on the return saves at least 0.5 mi. (0.8 km) and is a good introduction to some of the basics of safe, trailless route-finding. The overlook itself is exceptionally attractive, with an exciting final approach.

Trailhead: Heading north on NY 10, the trailhead is opposite a parking turnout on the east side of the road, just past the second bridge over the West Branch of the Sacandaga. From the south on NY 10, it is at a bend just before crossing the bridge. The sign at the trailhead on the west side of the road does not list Good Luck Cliffs, but does note routes to Good Luck Lake and Spectacle, Dry, and Dexter Lakes. These are snowmobile trails, wide and well-marked.

The trail climbs quite moderately for 0.3 mi. (0.5 km), then descends to reach a complex intersection at 0.5 mi. (0.8 km) with a trail register. (Note the trail that continues on to Dexter Lake. You will return along this trail if you opt to try the bushwhack return route.) Turn left at this intersection on the trail marked Good Luck Lake and Spectacle Lake. At first, the trail is mostly flat, with many wet spots. Then it descends, becoming less wet, and Good Luck Lake appears through the trees on the left. Several wet areas are spanned by short planks. At 1.4 mi. (2.2 km) the trail dips to a longer, more substantial bridge, beyond which the trail climbs a small knoll. Just before the

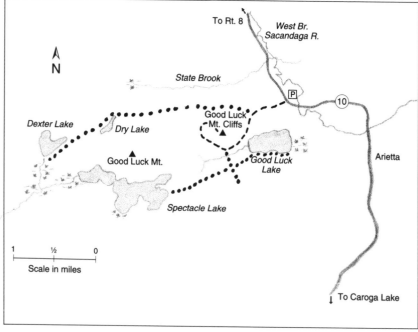

Good Luck Cliffs (54)

bridge the path to Good Luck Cliffs turns right. It is not marked. If you reach an intersecting trail for Spectacle Pond, you've gone too far. A large boulder is seen to the right as the trail begins.

The unmarked, but fairly easy to follow, path travels along the left bank of a small stream, crossing it shortly. The way heads up a ravine filled with many large boulders. A very large burl on a big maple tree may catch your attention. The path twists steeply upward, moving toward impressive cliffs on the right. At about 1.9 mi. (3.0 km) the path winds past boulders tumbled together and forming many small caves. A very large rock wall emerges through the trees on the right. The trail reaches a small flat area and crosses the stream. At 2.0 mi. (3.2 km) a tree marked by a ribbon and a large white painted dot marks the turn to the right that begins the final climb to the cliff tops, heading due north at first. Watch for an indistinct fork in the path at 2.1 mi. (3.4 km). The main path goes slightly left, though the right fork rejoins the path in 0.2 mi. (0.3 km). The climbing continues, with a large wall (the northwestern flank of the cliffs) on the right. The path levels off at 2.3 mi. (3.7 km). It then turns right for the final climb and then traverses the ridge to the top of the cliffs at 2.5 mi. (4.0 km). The drop-off is steep and dramatic, so hold on to young hikers and don't allow horseplay by the older hikers. The views to the west and southwest are truly spectacular. Spectacle Lake is prominent.

An alternative return route is highly recommended to avoid the steeper, wet sections of the path. It could be a good choice for a first bushwhack experience, but compass and trail map are recommended. After descending the first steep pitch from the ridge, take a bearing due north or just slightly east of north for a bushwhack to the snowmobile trail that runs east–west to Dexter Lake (noted earlier in this description). At first the descent is gradual, but it quickly grows steeper, and care should be taken to avoid a few sharp drops. For kids used to always being on a trail it can be exciting to break loose, in a way. A look at the trail map shows that any reasonably northward course will intersect the wide unmistakable snowmobile trail to Dexter Lake. Turn right (east) when you hit the snowmobile trail to rejoin the route taken in from the intersection with the trail register.

> *Many technical rock climbers try their skills on the rock wall below the cliffs. It may be fun to watch for a while if someone is climbing that day.*
> *We hiked this trail in the fall and passed much time on the*

*flatter sections giving smaller trees a gentle push to let some of
the dry leaves fall. Then we would see how many could be
caught in midair for good luck.*

55. Puffer Pond

Round-trip: 3.8 mi. (6.1 km)
Elevation change: 460 ft. (140 m)
Map: Bullhead 7.5', Thirteenth Lake 15',
    or Thirteenth Lake metric

This is a hike that provides a sense of real remoteness. The sign at
the trailhead indicates that the pond is 2.4 mi. (3.8 km) away, but the
correct distance is 1.9 mi. (3.0 km).

Trailhead: The trail begins from the east end of the parking area at
Kings Flow. From the intersection of NY 28 and NY 30 in Indian
Lake Village, drive south 0.6 mi. (1.0 km) on NY 30. Turn left onto
Big Brook Road. After 1.2 mi. (1.9 km) you'll cross a bridge at Lake
Abanakee. Bear right at the fork, 2.1 mi. (3.4 km) past Lake Abana-
kee. At the crossroads intersection with Hutchins and Moulton
Roads, turn right. Finally at 8.9 mi. (14.2 km) after leaving NY 30,
you reach Chimney Mountain Wilderness Lodge on Kings Flow.
This is private property, which the owner permits the public to cross
to reach the trails on state land beyond. A small parking fee is
requested.

The trail is a bit overgrown in places, but easy to follow. A few wet
spots and many small stream crossings slow the pace for the first
mile. The stream crossings were not difficult in mid-July but may be
more time-consuming in late spring. Shortly after 1.0 mi., the trail
diverges right from the brook it has been following, and begins a
moderately steep climb. The climb is steady, passing a junction for
the trail to John Pond at 1.2 mi. (1.9 km). In another 0.3 mi. (0.5 km)
the height of land is reached, then descends about 0.4 mi. (0.6 km)
to the shore of Puffer Pond. A lean-to is straight ahead, with another
down the trail 0.3 mi. (0.5 km) to the east. The return to the parking
area is quicker than the hike in, dropping some 460 ft. (140 m) from
the high point.

*The first lean-to is on high ground with a fine view across the
pond. This is a charming spot. The bowl-like hills around the*

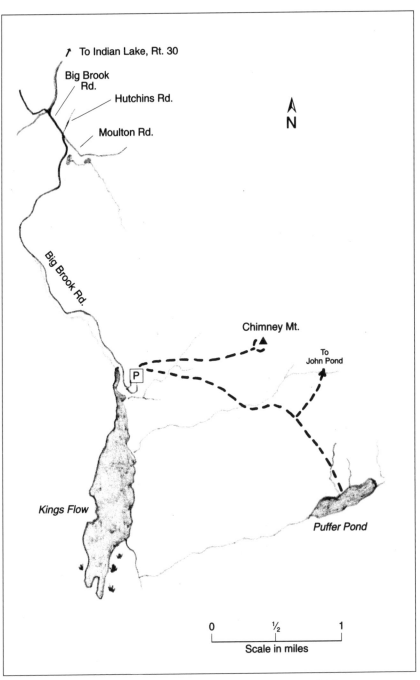

Puffer Pond (55) and Chimney Mountain (56)

*pond magnify the bird calls and hold the early morning mist so
even late-risers may catch a glimpse of it. We were lucky to have
three loons as our hosts, though they paid us very little heed. We
waded out from the sandy shore in front of the lean-to for a
swim. Newts were in abundance near shore. Don't be in a hurry;
it takes time to appreciate all that is here.*

*Camping in a lean-to in late summer, when the bugs aren't so
bad, is quite enjoyable. There isn't that confining feeling the tent
can sometimes bring. Watching the last glows of the embers and
feeling the night air on your face make drifting off to sleep quite
memorable. The eastward-facing lean-to means an early greet-
ing from the sun.*

*An activity that quickened the pace on the way out was for
each of us to guess our time of arrival at the trailhead. We
already knew what the trail was going to be like. We started
when we knew we had only 1.2 mi. (1.9 km) to the trailhead. This
type of contest helps develop a sense of estimating times based
on trail conditions.*

56. Chimney Mountain

Round-trip: 2.8 mi. (4.5 km)
Elevation change: 760 ft. (232 m)
Map: Bullhead Mountain 7.5', Thirteenth Lake 15', or Thirteenth
Lake metric

Among Adirondack peaks, this one is unique. (See map, page 145.) It
will be a favorite for most young hikers. A word of caution, though:
the cliffs and caves that make this hike attractive also pose dangers.
This is not a place for a toddler to scramble freely, and children of
every age should be impressed with the need to be careful.

Trailhead: The trail begins from the east end of the parking area at
Kings Flow. From the intersection of NY 28 and NY 30 in Indian
Lake Village, drive south 0.6 mi. (1.0 km) on NY 30. Turn left onto
Big Brook Road. After 1.2 mi. (1.9 km) you cross a bridge at Lake
Abanakee. Bear right at the fork, 2.1 mi. (3.4 km) past Lake Abanakee. At the crossroads intersection with Hutchins and Moulton
Roads, turn right. Finally, 8.9 mi. (14.2 km) after leaving NY 30, you
reach Chimney Mountain Wilderness Lodge on Kings Flow. This is
private property, which the owner permits the public to cross to
reach the trails on state land beyond. A small fee for parking is
requested.

A sign indicates 1.3 mi. (2.1 km) to the top of Chimney Mountain, which begins with an easy walk in open woods, crossing a brook within the first few hundred yards. The trail register is located at the start of state land, at about 0.4 mi. (0.6 km). Crossing another stream, the trail begins the first of several steeper sections. A long stretch of stone steps ("the gnome trail") testifies to the trail work that has been done here. Rocks with a very large vein of quartz can be seen on the right at about 0.7 mi. (1.1 km). A very steep section is encountered; at the top, the first of many informal paths leads left into an area of many caves. It would be best to skip these for now and continue on the main trail to the impressive rock towers at the top. Just prior to reaching them, there is a large camping area just off the trail to the right. At about the same point a path left descends to another path beneath the spires and the "chimney." The actual summit of the mountain is a bushwhack to the east, and not the main attraction. The marked trail leads straight to an incredible fairyland of layered rock spires. Some fine views, especially to the southwest over Kings Flow are had from parts of the rocky top. Can you see the car in the parking area?

The caves to the west of the main trail are worth a visit on the return trip. You can strike off on one of the many paths bearing southwest from the top. These paths thread their way through the caves, and eventually bend east to rejoin the main trail. A less venturesome approach would be to stay on the marked trail several hundred yards down, looking for one of the prominent paths to the right. Follow the paths to the caves, then retrace your way to the trail.

The many incredible rock formations at the top are irresistible for young would-be rock climbers. An easy scramble up may be followed by fear as they try to get back down. Extreme care should be taken here. Let children explore, as their abilities permit. Stay close to children whenever they are scrambling on the rocks.

Lake George & Southeast Section

Easy access to this corner of the Park by way of the Northway has contributed to rather intense development in some spots. Lake George Village is a center for tourist attractions. Even so, some outstanding backcountry hiking and camping can yet be found in this region. These trails do tend to be heavily used, but many remain in good condition, and the views they afford are among the best in the Park.

The Tongue Mountain area is home to the endangered eastern timber rattlesnake. Although venomous, the snakes are not aggressive and seldom seen. They may come out on a warm spring day to sun themselves. Observe caution and simply stay clear of their path. The snakes go to sleep for their winter hibernation as soon as the weather becomes cold.

OTHER ATTRACTIONS IN THIS SECTION:

- Adirondack Mountain Club Headquarters Information Center (518-668-4447)
- Fort Ticonderoga, Ticonderoga (518-585-2821)
- Fort William Henry, Lake George (518-668-5471)
- Lake George Arts Project, Lake George Village; cultural information (518-668-2616)
- Water Slide World, Lake George (518-668-4407)
- Up Yonda Farm, Bolton Landing; offers nature programs, butterfly house, and self-guided nature trail (518-644-9767)
- Penfield Museum, Ironville (518-597-3804)
- Public Campgrounds (call 1-800-456-2267 for reservations)

  Eagle Point—on Schroon Lake
  Hearthstone Point—north of Lake George Village
  Lake George Battleground—south of Lake George Village
  Luzerne—NY 9N southwest of Lake George Village
  Paradox Lake—east of Severance
  Putnam Pond—near Ticonderoga
  Rogers Rock—Hague

57. Shelving Rock Falls

Round-trip: about 1.0 mi. (1.6 km)
Elevation change: Minimal
Map: Shelving Rock 7.5'

It's a long drive into this falls, but if you are hiking Sleeping Beauty Mountain or are in the area it is worth the trip. This is a popular place in the summer and on weekends. Camping is permitted, but is restricted to the twenty-one designated campsites along the road

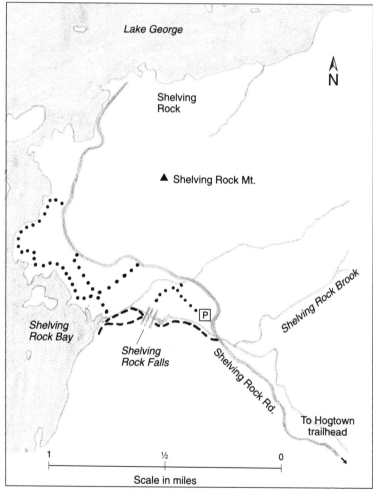

Shelving Rock Falls (57)

just north of the bridge over Shelving Rock Brook. Parking is restricted to the parking areas.

Trailhead: The Hogtown Trailhead parking area is a fairly long drive from any major highway. From NY 149, about midway between US 9 to the west and Fort Ann on US 4 to the east, turn north on the Buttermilk Falls Road. In 3.2 mi. (5.1 km) it bears left and becomes Sly Pond Road; the pavement ends shortly thereafter. At 8.7 mi. (13.9 km), Hogtown Road enters on the right. Go straight ahead on Shelving Rock Road and at 9.4 mi. (15.0 km) you will see the Hogtown trailhead parking lot ahead. Turn left on the road before the parking lot. The sign indicates Shelving Rock Mountain and Buck Mountain. Drive carefully down this road for 2.5 mi. (4.0 km). There will be a bridge over Shelving Rock Brook. A parking area is located just beyond the bridge on the left.

This walk is along an unmarked path that follows the brook to the falls. To begin, return to the south side of the bridge on the left bank of the brook. The trail is pretty level here as it follows the brook. In a short while the top of the falls is reached. The dam at the top of the falls is algae-covered and slippery. Do not walk on it. You will notice a path that descends to the base of the falls. The route continues down through the rocky gorge past swirling pools of water under towering trees. The path is eroded in many places and footing is not always great. You may want to keep a firm hold of a young child's hand. After about a half mile of scrambling along the shore you will reach a bridge where the brook enters into Shelving Rock Bay. Retrace your steps to return. *Guide to Adirondack Trails: Eastern Region* (see Selected References) describes longer hiking possibilities that continue along Shelving Rock Bay after crossing this lower bridge.

58. Crane Mountain

Round-trip: 2.8 mi. (4.5 km)
Round-trip loop: 3.6 mi. (5.8 km)
Elevation change: 1154 ft. (352 m)
Map: Johnsburg 7.5' or North Creek 15'

Many miles of marked trails make this a mountain of many opportunities and pleasures. Several different loops are possible, but
Crane Mountain is a steep climb however it's approached. It is not a
hike for beginners. The shortest route is up the east trail, 1.4 mi.
(2.2 km) to the summit, and back down the same way. We describe
a loop hike that includes a visit to Crane Mountain Pond.

Trailhead: Take NY 8 southwest from its intersection with NY 28 in
Wevertown. After about 2.0 mi. (3.2 km), head south on South
Johnsburg Road. Take Garnet Lake Road (west) from the hamlet of
Thurman. Proceed 1.4 mi. (2.2 km) to a right turn marked with a
DEC yellow and brown trail sign pointing the way to Crane Moun-
tain. This section of road is dirt and may be rough, especially in the
spring.

The sign at the trailhead indicates 1.8 mi. (2.9 km) to the summit by
the right fork of the two trails starting here. The correct distance is
1.4 mi. (2.2 km). Climbing begins almost immediately and is very
steep in places. At about 0.7 mi. (1.1 km) the trail to Crane Mountain
Pond enters on the left. Continuing right, you reach a short ladder
to help you ascend an expanse of rock with no hand or footholds.
The trail turns left, to a lovely glade. At 1.1 mi. (1.8 km) climbing
begins again and at 1.2 mi. (1.9 km) a long ladder ascends through a
dramatic break in the rock. Reaching the top, you are only a few
minutes' easy walk from the summit. The views are fine, especially
to the south. The trail heads northwest along mostly open rock,
descending gradually. In about 0.2 mi. (0.3 km) a short path left
leads to a beautiful overlook with Crane Mountain Pond several
hundred feet below. A steep descent through thick woods leads to a
junction very near the pond. The descent has some very steep and
potentially slippery sections, and the trail that continues along the
pond can be wet if beaver activity has raised the pond level. About
0.4 mi. (0.6 km) along the southern end of the pond, turn left on the
connector trail to complete the loop. The initial trail is rejoined
0.6 mi. (1.0 km) from the trailhead, making a 3.6-mi. (5.8-km) loop.

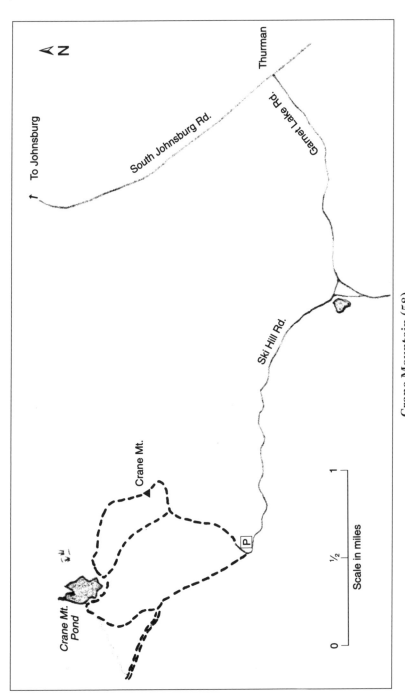

Crane Mountain (58)

Crane Mountain offers many other side trails and bushwhacks well worth exploring. See *Guide to Adirondack Trails: Southern Region*. It is a mountain that can be visited many times.

> *How are hikers' energy levels? Our boys decided to keep us informed of their energy levels on this hike by calling out numbers between one and one hundred, one hundred being fully charged. Hiking can both use up and restore energy. Steep or difficult parts reduce the number of "energies" on hand, but views, rest stops, and, through kid-logic, ladders and other unusual features, can replenish the supply. Crane Mountain has enough of the energy-restoring qualities to help make it a good kid hike, but this is not a beginner peak. The child with some hiking experience and acceptance of the need to persevere for promised rewards will enjoy this mountain.*

59. Hadley Mountain

Round-trip: 3.6 mi. (5.8 km)
Elevation change: 1500 ft. (457 m)
Map: Conklingville 7.5′and Stony Creek 7.5′,
　　or Lake Luzerne 15′

While 1500 ft. (457 m) is a serious ascent, the trail up Hadley is rarely steep. This is an excellent beginning peak and is, in fact, the first one our oldest son climbed on his own two feet. The views are among the best in the southern Adirondacks.

Trailhead: From NY 9N in Lake Luzerne, turn west through the town and cross the Hudson River to the adjoining town of Hadley. Head north on Stony Creek Road for approximately 3.0 mi. (4.8 km) to Hadley Hill Road. Turn left and drive 4.6 mi. (7.4 km) turning onto Tower Road on the right. The trail begins at 1.5 mi. (2.4 km) on the left at a parking area.

The red marked trail climbs steadily for the first 1.5 mi. (2.4 km). The walking is pleasant, sometimes on bare rock, sometimes through scattered boulders. A small stream is crossed at 0.5 mi. (0.8 km). At 0.6 mi. (1.0 km) some interesting rocks appear on the right.

The top of West Mountain Ridge (of which Hadley is a part) is reached at 1.0 mi. (1.6 km), and the trail turns right and climbs along the ridge crest. The walking is more open here and the grade more moderate. The trees along the ridge are stunted by their exposure to the wind and weather. At 1.3 mi. (2.1 km) the trail comes to a clearing. Two trails lead to the summit. The one to the left offers the best views along the way, with the first a fine lookout over Great Sacandaga Lake.

The path crosses many open areas in the final half mile to the summit. It is not necessary to climb the fire tower to enjoy unobstructed views in all directions. The tower has been restored (summer 1997) and the Fire Tower Committee has produced an educational brochure available at the trail register and through ADK and DEC.

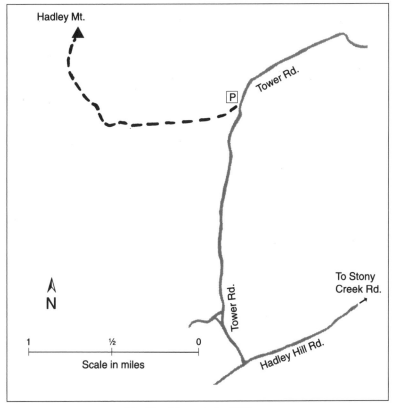

Hadley Mountain (59)

60. Black Mountain

Round-trip loop: 7.0 mi. (11.2 km)
Round-trip: 5.5 mi. (8.8 km)
Elevation change: 1000 ft. (305 m)
Map: Shelving Rock 7.5′ or Bolton Landing 15′

The best trail on Black Mountain is the one-mile climb up the south side. (See map, page 161.) The views along this trail are even better than those from the summit. The problem is finding a way to incorporate this trail into a day hike of reasonable length. Boating to Black Mountain Point, then hiking to the summit, is the shortest form of this hike, but the ascent is about 2300 ft. (701 m). An easier, though longer, way to proceed is to make a clockwise loop from the Pike Brook trailhead, past Lapland Pond and Black Mountain Ponds, over the summit and down the northeast side. It could also be done as a two-day trip for the experienced camper, camping at the lean-to or designated campsites by Black Mountain Ponds. The two-day trip provides a challenge because it involves carrying backpacks up and over the summit. When our boys were almost eight and ten years of age we completed the loop as a day trip with lots of rests along the way.

Trailhead: From NY 22 turn west at the sign for Hulett's Landing and drive 2.7 mi. (4.3 km), then turn left onto Pike Brook Road. At 0.8 mi. (1.3 km), the trailhead parking lot and trail register are on the right.

Follow red trail markers along a rough road. It can be very muddy. In fact, much of the first mile is especially attractive to those who love the sound of boots sucking mud. (Ways to avoid mud are also present.) At 0.5 mi. (0.8 km) an old farmhouse and barn are passed on the left. At 1.2 mi. (1.9 km) there is a junction (the sign is high on a tree). To hike Black Mountain as a loop, turn left here, toward Lapland Pond. This trail is more pleasant, passing through hemlock woods with a beaver pond to the right. At 2.0 mi. (3.2 km) the trail crosses a "billy goat" bridge over the beaver pond outlet, with a good view of the cliffs of Black Mountain across the pond.

The trail crosses and recrosses (rock hopping) a stream before turning away. Soon the trail starts descending toward Lapland Lake. At 2.1 mi. (3.4 km) there is a junction with a spur trail down the east shore of Lapland Lake to a lean-to (0.2 mi. [0.3 km]). It is nicely

situated behind open rock sloping into the pond. Continue on the main trail for 2.3 mi. (3.7 km) to the junction with Black Mountain Pond. The trail goes right and becomes drier. At 2.5 mi. (4.0 km) the first of the two ponds appears on the left. A camping area is just off the trail on the right.

After passing this pond, the trail crosses an inlet brook and climbs a ridge. At 2.9 mi. (4.6 km) it reaches the second pond and lean-to. The lean-to sits at the top of a rock slab facing south, with a nice view to the marshy southern shore of the pond. This is a nice rest spot. Watch for newts at the water's edge.

The trail continues below the lean-to close to the shore of the pond and at 3.3 mi. (5.3 km) reaches a junction with the red marked trail up Black Mountain. Turning right here, the trail is well designed and maintained. It's the very model of a steep trail that is so well graded and interesting that it seems easy. Lots of switchbacks keep the grade moderate, and progressively more expansive views of Lake George to the west greet you. Some spots are quite steep and rocky. This is climbing!

At 4.1 mi. (6.6 km) a side trail on the right leads to a grassy clearing and ledges with a view of Lake George and its many islands. The remaining trail to the summit is more gentle. The summit at 4.3 mi. (6.9 km) is topped by a windmill that generates power for a communication antenna. The windmill is surrounded by cyclone fencing and can be pretty noisy. The observer's cabin is still there and from a grassy open area in front of it there are good views north along Lake George.

To complete the loop, follow the red marked trail down the east side. After a sharp right turn the trail is often in a streambed and can be very wet. Snowmobile trails intersect the main trail. Take care to follow the red markers. The trail crosses several nice brooks. From the summit it is 1.5 mi. (2.4 km) to the junction with the trail to Lapland Lake. Continue straight at this junction (on the trail and road on which you came in) to reach the parking lot in another 1.2 mi. (1.9 km).

> *This hike clearly demonstrated to us that young children derive pleasure in very different ways from adults. As we diligently looked for rock steps and carefully placed logs in the muddy sections to keep our boots reasonably clean and dry, our children decided they'd had enough of avoiding mud and tramped down the middle of the trail no matter what, chanting, "We are soldiers of the trail." What joy it was for them to slosh through mud and water six or more inches deep! We laughed hearing their shrieks of laughter. Their enjoyment was well worth the extra cleanup effort. Remember, though, that wet feet on a cool day can quickly lower your child's body temperature.*

61. Sleeping Beauty Mountain

Round-trip from Dacy Clearing: 3.6 mi. (5.8 km)
Round-trip from Hogtown Trailhead: 6.8 mi. (10.9 km)
Elevation change: 1000 ft. (305 m)
Map: Shelving Rock 7.5'

This is a real fairy-tale mountain. One could easily imagine oneself a king or queen surveying the realm from the ramparts of its rocky summit. Although the trail is short there is a significant ascent. It's a good trail, however, with lots of switchbacks to make the grade less rigorous.

Trailhead: The Hogtown Trailhead parking area is a fairly long drive from any major highway. From NY 149, about midway between US 9 to the west and Fort Ann on US 4 to the east, turn north on the Buttermilk Falls Road. In 3.2 mi. (5.1 km) it bears left and becomes

Sly Pond Road; the pavement ends shortly thereafter. Continuing on the dirt road, Hogtown Road enters on the right at 8.7 mi. (13.9 km). Go straight ahead on Shelving Rock Road and at 9.4 mi. (15.0 km) you will come to the Hogtown Trailhead parking lot. During dry season you can continue through this parking area along a very small and somewhat rough dirt road for 1.6 mi. (2.6 km) to the parking area at Dacy Clearing. A barrier with a stop sign marks the start of the yellow marked trail up Sleeping Beauty.

The trail begins on the road beyond the barrier. A stream parallels the trail on the right. A small stream is crossed and recrossed as the old road climbs gently to a trail junction in a flat area at 0.6 mi.

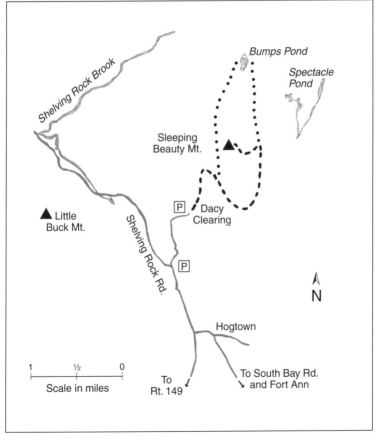

Sleeping Beauty Mountain (61)

(1.0 km). Turn right for the most direct trail to Sleeping Beauty. The trail heads south for a short while, then turns east. Immense cliffs appear ahead through the trees at 1.0 mi. (1.6 km). The trail is skirting the south face of Sleeping Beauty. Soon turning northeast, the trail reaches the first switchback past a small ledge. The trail gets steeper as it circles more to the north, then flattens out. At 1.7 mi. (2.7 km) there is an indistinct junction with the less used trail to the right leading to Bumps Pond. On the return, be careful to take the right fork here.

The burst onto the summit at 1.8 mi. (2.9 km) is one of the best surprises in the Adirondacks. The rocky knob is completely bare and offers superb views of Lake George, Tongue Mountain and the southern Adirondack peaks. Lots of scrambling possibilities beckon, but be aware of the dangerous drops on many sides.

62. Tongue Mountain Lean-to and Five Mile Mountain

Round-trip to Tongue Mountain lean-to:
    5.2 mi. (8.3 km)
Elevation change: 940 ft. (287 m)
Round-trip to Five Mile Mountain: 7.0 mi. (11.2 km)
Elevation change: 1090 ft. (332 m)
Map: Silver Bay 7.5' or Bolton Landing 15'

Many interesting trails lace this large block of state land extending into Lake George. From the north trailhead on NY 9N to the tip of the "tongue" (Montcalm Point) is 11.2 mi. (17.9 km), but many points along the way are suitable destinations, depending on the stamina of your hikers and the amount of time available. Tongue Mountain lean-to at 2.6 mi. (4.2 km) is a fine picnic spot, and a round-trip to it is very rewarding. Continuing 0.9 mi. (1.4 km) to Five Mile Point is fairly easy walking, often on open ridge top, with a few steep sections. This would increase the round-trip distance to 7.0 mi. (11.2 km). See note about rattlesnakes in this area on p. 149.

Trailhead: From exit 24 on the Northway, drive east toward Bolton Landing. At the junction with NY 9N turn north and drive 9.5 mi. (15.2 km) to a parking area for the north trailhead for the Tongue Mountain Range.

The trail begins along an old road, parallel to NY 9N, heading west. At 0.1 mi. (0.2 km) the register is at a turn to the left as the trail leaves the road. In wet weather the trail is very muddy and is rather eroded. As the trail turns to the southeast it begins to climb and becomes drier. At 0.5 mi. (0.8 km) it crosses a small stream and curves more to the east. The junction with the trail to Deer Leap (yellow markers) is at 0.6 mi. (1.0 km). This 1.1-mi. (1.8-km) spur trail is a very popular one, leading to some nice views over Lake George.

The trail along the Tongue Mountain Ridge goes right and continues as a very pleasant walk through oak woods, with moderate climbs alternating with flatter walking. At 1.7 mi. (2.7 km) there is a

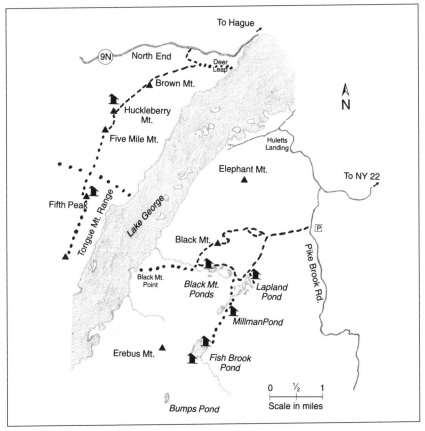

**Black Mountain (60) and Tongue Mountain Lean-to
and Five Mile Mountain (62)**

lookout just off the trail on the left. On a clear day, with binoculars, one can see the windmill on top of Black Mountain.

Just beyond a clearing at 1.9 mi. (3.0 km) the trail turns sharply left to skirt a rock outcrop. It crosses a small stream and begins to climb again. Many rock cairns dot the way during the ascent to the lean-to (without a floor) at 2.6 mi. (4.2 km). There are fine views to the north and many open areas suitable for picnicking. Lichen- and moss-covered rocks are particularly abundant. Care should be taken to stay on bare rock as much as possible.

The trail continues past the lean-to with much more open rock underfoot. Cairns mark the trail, which descends at 3.3 mi. (5.3 km) and then climbs up and over the ledges near the summit of Five Mile Mountain at 3.5 mi. (5.6 km).

> *In the fall, this is a great hike on which to go in search of the "perfect" acorn — one with a cap firmly attached. You may also find many acorns with small holes, a sign of the acorn weevil. Oaks are long-lived trees and don't produce acorns until they are at least twenty years old. They will often live to be 100 years old.*

Selected References

Travel and Visitor Information

DeLorme Mapping Co. *New York State Atlas and Gazetteer.* Freeport, Maine: DeLorme Mapping Co., 1988.

Road maps just don't give the detail you sometimes need to locate a trailhead. This collection of topographic maps of the entire state is an excellent reference.

Folwell, Elizabeth. *The Adirondack Book: A Complete Guide,* 2d ed. Stockbridge, Massachussets: Berkshire House Publishers, 1996.

A very thorough guide with information on places to eat and sleep, museums, golf courses, attractions. Complete with phone numbers and addresses.

Guides to the Trails

Adirondack Mountain Club. *Guide to Adirondack Trails,* Forest Preserve Series, 2d ed. 8 volumes. Lake George, New York: Adirondack Mountain Club, 1994.

These seven volumes, vetted by rangers and updated regularly, cover all trails throughout the Adirondack Park. They are subtitled by region: High Peaks, Northern, Central, Northville-Placid Trail, West-Central, Eastern, and Southern. The eighth volume is *Guide to Catskill Trails.*

Wadsworth, Bruce. *An Adirondack Sampler: Day Hikes for All Seasons,* 4th ed. Lake George, New York: Adirondack Mountain Club, 1996.

Wadsworth, Bruce. *An Adirondack Sampler 2: Backpacking Trips for All Seasons,* 2d ed. Lake George, New York: Adirondack Mountain Club, 1995.

Field Guides to Help You Name and Understand What You See

Amsel, Sheri. *Adirondack Nature Guide: A Field Guide to Birds, Mammals, Trees, Insects, Wildflowers, Amphibians, Reptiles, and Where To Find Them.* Mt. Kisco, New York: Pinto Press, 1997.

Bessette, Alan E. *Mushrooms of the Adirondacks: A Field Guide.* Utica, New York: North Country Books, 1988.

Durell, Gerald. *The Amateur Naturalist.* New York: Alfred A. Knopf, 1982.

Not so much an identification book as one that teaches you how to be a naturalist, what to look for and how to observe.

Forey, Pamela, and Cecilia Fitzsimons. *An Instant Guide to Reptiles and Amphibians.* New York: Crescent Books, 1987.

Hallowell, Anne and Barbara Hallowell. *Fern Finder: A Guide to Native Ferns of Northeastern and Central North America.* Berkeley, California: Nature Study Guild, 1981.

Lawrence, Eleanor and Sue Harniess. *An Instant Guide to Mushrooms & Other Fungi.* New York: Crescent Books, 1991.

Ketchledge, E. H. *Forests & Trees of the Adirondack High Peaks Region: A Hiker's Guide*, 3d ed. Lake George, New York: Adirondack Mountain Club, 1996.

McGrath, Anne. *Wildflowers of the Adirondacks.* Utica, New York: North Country Books, 1981.

Niering, William A. *The Audubon Society Nature Guides: Wetlands.* New York: Alfred A. Knopf, 1987.

Palmer, Laurence and H. Seymour Fowler. *Fieldbook of Natural History*, 2d ed. New York: McGraw-Hill Book Co., 1975.

This book is now out of print, but is an excellent reference if you can locate it in a library or used bookstore.

The Peterson First Guides Series. Boston: Houghton Mifflin Co.

This series includes guides to butterflies, birds, and wildflowers. They are simplified from the adult versions and much easier for children to use.

Schottman, Ruth. *Trailside Notes: A Naturalist's Companion to Adirondack Plants.* Lake George, New York: Adirondack Mountain Club, 1997.

Slack, Nancy and Allison Bell. *85 Acres: A Field Guide to the Adirondack Alpine Summits.* Lake George, New York: Adirondack Mountain Club, 1993.

VanDiver, Brad. *Rocks and Routes of the North Country: New York.* Geneva, New York: W. F. Humphrey Press, Inc., 1976.

A guide to geology and mineral collecting in the Adirondacks and the St. Lawrence Valley.

Books Written for Children to Read

Aronsky, Jim. *Crinklefoot's Guide to Walking in Wild Places.* New York: Bradbury Press, 1990.

This book is now out of print, but is an excellent reference if you can locate it in a library or used bookstore. Crinklefoot is a fictional character born in a tree and raised by bees. Lots of commonsense information is contained within the pages of this delightful picture book.

Aronsky, Jim. *Crinklefoot's Guide to Knowing the Trees.* New York: Bradbury Press, 1992.

This book is now out of print, but is an excellent reference if you can locate it in a library or used bookstore. Crinklefoot will leave any child with a better understanding and appreciation of trees.

McMartin, Barbara. *Adventures in Hiking: A Young Peoples' Guide to the Adirondacks.* Utica, New York: North Country Books, 1993.

A guide to twenty-eight hikes, written for the young hiker. Includes some trails not found in this book.

Silver, Donald M. *One Small Square: Woods.* New York: W. H. Freeman & Co., 1995.

The author invites children to become "detectives" within a small square they mark in the woods. They are given a variety of activities to try that give clues to the seasonal changes and occurrences within their square.

Steinberg, Michael. *Our Wilderness: How the People of New York Found, Changed and Preserved the Adirondacks.* Lake George, New York: Adirondack Mountain Club, 1992.

An entertaining and informative history for readers aged 10 and up.

Books that Tell the "How To's" of Hiking

Brown, Tom. *Tom Brown's Field Guide to Nature and Survival for Children.* New York: Berkley Publishing Group, 1989.

McManners, Hugh. *The Complete Wilderness Training Book: Field Skills for Adventure in the Outdoors.* New York: Dorling Kindersley Publishing, Inc., 1994.

Well-illustrated guide to survival and general practice in the backcountry.

Randall, Joseph. *The Modern Backpacker's Handbook.* New York: Lyons & Burford, 1994.

A good basic text on the practice of hiking and camping.

Ross, Cindy and Todd Gladfelter. *A Hiker's Companion: Twelve Thousand Miles of Trail-Tested Wisdom.* Seattle, Washington: Mountaineer Books, 1993.

Anecdotes and advice from two people who have really tested their ideas.

Ross, Cindy and Todd Gladfelter. *Kids in the Wild: A Family Guide to Outdoor Recreation.* Seattle, Washington: Mountaineer Books, 1995.

This book covers many different outdoor activities, with emphasis on how to manage when children are included.

Books that Would Appeal to Teachers As Well As Parents

Cornell, Joseph B. *Sharing Nature with Children: A Parents' and Teachers' Nature-Awareness Guidebook.* Nevada City, California: Ananda Publications, 1979.

This small book suggests many activities for introducing children to nature.

Carson, Rachel. *The Sense of Wonder.* New York: Harper and Row, 1956.

An inspiring book about why it's important to keep alive a sense of wonder within children.

Outreach Materials and Programs.
A pamphlet prepared by the Adirondack Mountain Club Education Department, P.O. Box 867, Lake Placid, New York 12946. Includes information on how to obtain teacher kits, slide sets, and videotapes on various outdoor activities (hiking, skiing, etc.) and wilderness topics.

Other Good Books to Read

Abram, David. *The Spell of the Sensuous: Perception in Language in a More Than Human World.* New York: Pantheon Books, 1996.

DiNunzio, Michael G. *Adirondack Wildguide: A Natural History of the Adirondack Park.* Keene Valley, New York: The Adirondack Nature Conservancy and Adirondack Council, 1984.

Jamieson, Paul. *The Adirondack Reader.* Lake George, New York: Adirondack Mountain Club, 1982.

Orr, David W. *Earth in Mind: On Education, Environment, and the Human Prospect.* Washington D.C.: Island Press, 1994.

Essays on how we could be doing a better job of educating our youth about environmental issues, and why it is important to do so.

Serrao, John. *Nature's Events: A Notebook of the Unfolding Seasons.* Mechanicsburg, Pennsylvania: Stackpole Books, 1992.

A nice discussion of 48 seasonal "mileposts," each a short study of recurring natural phenomena over the course of the year.

Terrie, Philip G. *Wildlife and Wilderness: A History of Adirondack Mammals.* Fleischmanns, New York: Purple Mountain Press, 1993.

This short book describes a complex, often conflict-ridden relationship.

Graham, Frank. *The Adirondack Park: A Political History.* New York: Alfred A. Knopf, 1978.

A history of the park from first encounters by Europeans to contemporary controversies.

Sources of Additional Information

Adirondack Mountain Club
Headquarters Information Center
814 Goggins Rd.
Lake George, N.Y. 12845-4117
518-668-4447

The Adirondack Museum
P.O. Box 99
Blue Mountain Lake, N.Y. 12812
518-352-7311

The Adirondack Nature
Conservancy
P.O. Box 65
Keene Valley, N.Y. 12943
518-576-2082

*New York State Dept. of Environ-
mental Conservation*
www.dec.state.ny.us

Region 5

Ray Brook, N.Y.
518-897-1200

Northville, N.Y.
518-863-4545

Indian Lake, N.Y.
518-648-5616

Region 6

Potsdam, N.Y. (St. Lawrence Cty.)
315-265-3090

Herkimer, N.Y. (Herkimer Cty.)
315-866-6330

Lowville, N.Y. (Lewis Cty.)
315-376-3521

New York State Public
Campgrounds
Information: 518-457-2500
Reservations: 800-456-CAMP

Up Yonda Farm Environmental
Education Center
P.O. Box 1453
Bolton Landing, N.Y. 12814
518-644-9767/3823

Visitor Interpretive Centers

NY 30, Box 3000
Paul Smiths, N.Y. 12970
518-327-3000

NY 28N, Box 101
Newcomb, N.Y. 12852
518-582-2000

About the Authors

David and Rose live with their sons Albert, 10, and Willie, 8, in Potsdam, New York. David is a librarian at the State University of New York at Potsdam, and Rose teaches third and fourth graders at Parishville-Hopkinton Elementary School. The authors have been hiking together in the Adirondacks, Vermont, Maine, and the Dolomites of Italy for many years, the last ten in the company of one or both of their favorite hiking companions, Albert and Willie. Albert's experiences in the woods have provided inspiration for his drawings, and Willie's growing enthusiasm has him poring over maps, planning outings of impossibly many peaks and miles. Their four-legged companion Frodo, an enthusiastic hiker, is the newest addition to the family.

Photograph Locations

Index

Take the Kids Challenge!

For more information and a free brochure call ADK at 518-668-4447 or visit our Web site at www.adk.org.

Join Us!

We are a nonprofit membership organization that brings together people with interests in recreation, conservation, and environmental education in the New York State Forest Preserve.

Membership Benefits

Discovery

ADK can broaden your horizons by introducing you to new people, new places, recreational activities, and interests.

Member Benefits

- 20% discount on all ADK publications, including guidebooks and maps
- 10% discount on ADK lodging facilities in the Adirondacks
- 10% discount on ADK logo merchandise
- reduced rates on educational programs
- One-year subscription to *Adirondac* magazine
- Membership in one of ADK's 26 chapters
- Member-only outings to exciting destinations around the world

Satisfaction

Knowing you're doing your part to protect and preserve our mountains, rivers, forests, and lakes to ensure that future generations will be able to enjoy the wilderness as we have.

To Join:
Call 1-800-395-8080

☐ Family $45

☐ Adult $40

☐ Senior (65+) $30

☐ Junior (under 18) $25

All major credit cards accepted. Or, mail check or money order (U.S. funds only) with membership request to:

Adirondack Mountain Club
814 Goggins Road
Lake George, NY 12845-4117

All fees subject to change.   HWC